The Way *of* Awakening

OTHER BOOKS BY PAUL F. GORMAN

The Way *of* Awakening

PAUL F. GORMAN

VINE
PRESS

REDONDO BEACH
CALIFORNIA

The Way of Awakening

First edition 2012
Second edition 2014
Third edition 2016

Published by Vine Press
An imprint of Giving Self, Inc
2110 Artesia Boulevard 109, Redondo Beach, CA 90278

www.miracleself.com

ISBN-13: 978-0692642955
ISBN-10: 0692642951

Set in JansonURW 11/13
Printed by CreateSpace

Available worldwide from Amazon and all other book stores

Rise in consciousness—this is the entire secret.

As consciousness rises, detaching from and leaving behind false belief, ever greater degrees of heaven are visible through the unconditioned mind.

"As in heaven so on earth."

The earth and all its people, creatures and conditions are witnessed unconditioned, whole and harmonious, love and union of all emerging through the fog of false sense.

Indeed, "As in heaven so on earth" emerges as the one reality—the bondage of false material sense dispelled, the unconditioned experience of man, earth and universe harmonious, peaceful, purposeful and free, in love.

Edited by M.L.

Thank you for bringing your invaluable talent,
with so much love and dedication, to this text.

CONTENTS

IN THE BEGINNING

In the beginning the dawn of realization gently pene-
trates material sense. Spiritual awareness stirs within
the receptivity of being and five seeds of truth begin to
take root:

> The 'I' of being is not local, finite or temporal but
> infinite—infinity itself, the infinitude of truth *being*
> all that is.

> ~

> The truth of being—the pure and fulfilled 'I' of you,
> me and all—is omnipresent as each point of itself.
> The whole of God, spirit and truth, is omnipresent
> at every point of itself simultaneously.

> ~

> God is ever manifested, tangible and visible. There
> is no 'unmanifested, undemonstrated, intangible or
> invisible' God—spirit, truth.

> ~

> God is one, oneness. There is no other. There is
> not 'two' or 'twoness.' Nothing exists, anywhere,
> under any circumstance or condition but the one
> truth, the one infinity of being, body, thing,
> amount, activity and condition.

There is not God *and*. There is *just* God, *just* truth, *just* infinity, *just* wholeness and completeness of all everywhere present.

~

Because God is one *being* oneness, omnipresence *being* omnipresent, it does not and cannot *change* its substance, form, character, nature, presence into something it is not.

Oneness, omnipresence is itself alone, and forever remains itself alone "with none else."

Consider: where would 'change' happen, or exist, in one being oneness, in omnipresence *being* omnipresent?

The more we live with the awareness of this truth—which means constantly knowing and *being* these five aspects of truth rather than being a lesser degree of awareness which accepts material, physical, finite existence as being real—the more oneness, infinity and omnipresence of being we experience as real, tangible and practical in every situation and condition of daily experience.

MISTAKEN IDENTITY

Fundamentally, the only struggle we have as awakening beings, and the only struggle we experience with the material sense, is that of *mistaken identity*.

Because God—spirit and truth—is the only presence, the infinitude itself, you are that, I am that, and all is that. "I am" and "I am that" is the only truthful identity.

The more we seek truth in order to harmonize our

conceptual experience—and the more urgently we seek it because of a painful or fearful experience of illness, unhappiness, lack, limitation or insecurity—the more we chase that which we already, in truth, *are* and *have*. We chase the un-chase-able; therefore we fail.

It is in chasing the un-chase-able that we delay our truthful experience—the miracle of truth tangibly evident as our everyday conceptual harmony, health, wealth, peace, happiness and purpose—our true infinity, freedom and purpose of being.

Chasing truth is what we do by searching for *the secret* on page after page of spiritual books, by travelling the world in search of truth, by visiting holy places in hope of discovering truth there, by listening to endless truth classes, or attending endless live classes in the hope that *they*, or the *next one* will reveal the secret for which we search. We chase truth by latching onto truth statements trying to witness the truth they speak of, or trying to *make* their truth *work* in our experience. As we have each discovered by our own 'failure,' chasing truth does not, and cannot, work.

It is only as we come to realize that *we already are truth* and that everything everywhere already *is* and already contains *the fullness of truth* that we become still and quiet and are able to begin witnessing truth in and as our everyday experience.

THE WHOLE IS THE ONLY

Because truth is indivisible—because the whole exists at every point in and of infinity at the same time—*one* truth statement, any truth statement, is and contains the *whole truth*. Any *one* truth statement contains, and is itself, the *whole* secret of awakening.

We have failed to recognize this so we do not stick with

one or at most a handful of truth statements, deepening our understanding of each, enriching our awareness with the truth of which each speaks. Thereby we miss truth. We pass by the very truth we're seeking.

Yet enriching awareness by taking one or just a very few truth statements and really *working* with them, seeking the depth and richness of their truth, and letting that deeper truth awareness *be* or become evident in and as our experience, is the great key to illuminating individual and collective awareness, the key to spiritual awakening.

This enriching of awarenessness is what Jesus explains in the Parable of the Sower:

1 And again He began to teach by the sea. And a great multitude was gathered to Him, so that He got into a boat and sat in it on the sea; and the whole multitude was on the land facing the sea.

2 Then He taught them many things by parables, and said to them in His teaching:

3 Listen! Behold, a sower went out to sow.

4 And it happened, as he sowed, that some seed fell by the wayside; and the birds of the air came and devoured it.

5 Some fell on stony ground, where it did not have much earth; and immediately it sprang up because it had no depth of earth.

6 But when the sun was up it was scorched, and because it had no root it withered away.

7 And some seed fell among thorns; and the thorns grew up and choked it, and it yielded no crop.

8 But other seed fell on good ground and yielded a crop that sprang up, increased and produced: some thirtyfold, some sixty, and some a hundred.

9 And He said to them, He who has ears to hear, let

him hear!

10 But when He was alone, those around Him with the twelve asked Him about the parable.

11 And He said to them, To you it has been given to know the mystery of the kingdom of God; but to those who are outside, all things come in parables,

12 so that seeing they may see and not perceive, And hearing they may hear and not understand; Lest they should turn

13 And He said to them, Do you not understand this parable? How then will you understand all the parables?

14 The sower sows the word.

15 And these are the ones by the wayside where the word is sown. When they hear, Satan [material belief] comes immediately and takes away the word that was sown in their hearts.

16 These likewise are the ones sown on stony ground who, when they hear the word, immediately receive it with gladness;

17 and they have no root in themselves, and so endure only for a time. Afterward, when tribulation or persecution arises for the word's sake, immediately they stumble.

18 Now these are the ones sown among thorns; they are the ones who hear the word,

19 and the cares of this world, the deceitfulness of riches [material belief and desire], and the desires for other things entering in choke the word, and it becomes unfruitful.

20 But these are the ones sown on good ground, those who hear the word, accept it, and bear fruit: some thirtyfold, some sixty, and some a hundred.[1]

THE WAY: SPIRITUAL NOURISHMENT AND ENRICHMENT

The way of spiritual illumination is *depth* of truth awareness. It is the *spiritualizing* of awareness—of being. The depth of truth awareness we establish as the very essence of our being is the "good ground" the Master speaks of, which bears rich fruit (rich and harmonious experience)—"some thirtyfold, some sixty, and some a hundred."

We nourish and enrich our being by *deepening* truth awareness.

"Know the truth, and that very truth will set you free."[2] The Master is telling us: the greater *depth* and *specificity* of truth we know, the greater freedom and fruitage of life *as that very truth* we then experience.

Why? The degree or amount of truth we are aware of in a living way *is* tangible experience—tangible body, form, amount, activity, condition experienced. Spiritual awareness is itself the spiritual harmony and wholeness of experience. The more and deeper truth we have and are being, the more abundant, harmonious and true is our experience.

Remember: all is oneness *being* one existence, *one* in or as experience. That which seems to be 'inner' versus 'outer' *isn't*. All is one. Despite appearance and despite belief about appearance, the 'inner' and 'outer' are *one* not two—not different, not separate; neither two, different or separate *states of being.* Only God is, therefore only *one* is. And because only God (one) is, it can be understood that God

[1] Mark 4:1-20   [2] John 8:32

is mind *is* formation. Mind *is* all formation (universe-earth). That which appears to be God 'and' mind 'and' formation is actually one presence—*being* mind, *being* formation.

Mind does not 'produce' the formation and activity we call experience. Mind *is* the formation and activity of experience (earth-universe). And because only God is, it follows that mind is God (the only). It then follows that because mind is formation, all formation is God. Simply and clearly stated, God *is* mind *is* formation.[1]

God—consciousness, oneness—has no inner versus outer. When you peer into pure consciousness—pure oneness, pure presence—you find no difference or separation between that body or place or condition which appears to be taking place in the 'outer,' than you do in that which appears to be 'inner' or 'within.' *All is one and omnipresent* despite appearance.

God—consciousness—*is* the substance, form, body, amount, activity and condition we experience as our conceptual world. All formation is God-formation—whole, perfect, healthy, harmonious, purposeful and eternal. But individual and collective *awareness* of this great truth determines individual or collective *degrees of its experience.* Only that which we are *aware* of can be our experience—and inescapably *is.* You can see that if we have been given a gift of a new automobile yet are unaware of the gift, our experience does not, and cannot, include that automobile. But the moment we become aware of it we tangibly *have* it. It is now real, tangible and practical in our experience, but not before we are aware of it. This is the very same in truth. Only the truth we are *aware of* is the truth we experience—the only truth we *can* experience. Therefore, the greater *depth* of truth we have—we know—the greater depth of truth we evidence, as in the Parable of the Sower and the example of the automobile.

---

[1] For a more in-depth explanation of "God *is* mind *is* formation," see *The 7 Spiritual Steps To Solving Any Problem* by Paul F. Gorman

OUR WORK OF AWAKENING

For the rest of this book we will work with three primary truth statements over a period of twelve weeks. Work with each chapter for one whole week.

This first week we need to prepare and fertilize the soil of awareness in readiness for the "planting" of the three truth statements.

We prepare and fertilize awareness by deepening our understanding of what has been given us in these first pages. The *more deeply* we understand what has been explained above, the *more* prepared and fertilized becomes our being—our living awareness.

We want—as the Master shared—for our being, our awareness, to be the "good ground" that has depth and the nutrients of understanding and receptivity that yield rich fruitage—*"[This] seed fell on good ground and yielded a crop that sprang up, increased and produced: some thirtyfold, some sixty, and some a hundred."*

Read "In the Beginning" each day for the following week—maybe two or three times each day. Then take the message into meditation. Ponder it, begin to awaken to it, understand it, realize the truth you are receiving.

Interlace pondering with periods of silence so that the message (truth realization) takes root and grows—beginning to "increase and produce" a crop of truth that will spring up as your experience.

Devote three or four hours throughout each day to reading this message, meditating upon each chapter as you get to it, and to periods of silence, through and as which the message becomes the "image and likeness" of God as your experience—the good, harmonious and abundant form of everything of your life.

WEEKS ONE – THREE

❧

THE
FIRST
TRUTH

THE FIRST TRUTH

❧

With the previous seven days of preparing and enriching the soil (receptivity) of being—awareness—we are ready to plant our primary realizations of truth.

Perhaps the three most significant and 'complete' realizations of truth ever given mankind are the following (these particular statements are taken from the Bible, but in spiritual scripture the world over we find the same three truths revealed):

> "All things were made through him, and without him nothing was made that was made,"[1] and "God saw every thing that he had made, and, behold, it was very good."[2]

> "The earth is the Lord's, and the fullness thereof; the world, and they that dwell therein."[3] Therefore "I am that I am."[4]

> "Unless the Lord builds the house, they labor in vain that build it; unless the Lord guards the city, the watchman stays awake in vain."[5]

We are being given (planting) all three truths now so that they can each start taking root. We will be working with and expounding on these three throughout the book,

[1] John 1:3   [2] Genesis 1:31   [3] Psalm 24:1   [4] Exodus 3:14   [5] Psalm 127:1

allowing them to take *deep* root, grow, blossom and produce rich fruitage in individual experience and for the good of all.

We are working with the *first* truth alone this week (let the other two rest within you this week; no attention need be given them).

THE FIRST TRUTH

"All things were made through Him, and without Him nothing was made that was made," and "God saw every thing that he had made, and, behold, it was very good."

We must take truth *literally.* Truth must become a living, moving *reality* to us and as us. Truth must become what we are *in living awareness.*

Of course, truth *is already* what we are, but because truth, God, the infinite, is *consciousness,* the entire 'secret' is *conscious awareness* of who and what we truly are and have.

Always, it is about being *consciously aware.*

Truth is true; truth is the one, therefore *only* reality. But unless and until we each become (awaken) *consciously aware* of truth being what and who we are, and what all is, then the boundless, limitless resources and fulfillment of being cannot be tangibly evident in and as our experience.

Here's a good example. We recently took a trip to Boulder, Colorado for a few days. We love vegetarian food, and so we looked for a nice restaurant as we explored downtown and the charming Pearl Street Mall. No vegetarian restaurant anywhere in sight.

Well, after a wonderful first day's visit we decided to head back to our hotel. Just as we were within 50 yards of the front door *there was a first class vegetarian restaurant!*

We had walked right past it on our way in and out of our hotel, but we had no *conscious awareness* of its presence; therefore it 'did not exist tangibly' in our experience.

It was *there*, tangibly and visibly. Yet without our *conscious awareness*, it was 'not there'; it was 'intangible and invisible.' It is only 'there' for those who are *consciously aware* of its presence. The very moment we became *consciously* aware of it, it was tangible and visible as our immediate fulfillment of experience.

This is *exactly* what happens as we awaken to any aspect of life. All awakening is the same thing—the awakening to more of the truth that forever stands all about us, fully tangible and visible, fully real and practical.

All is God: "All things were made through Him, and without Him nothing was made that was made"; therefore, everything everywhere without exception (in our case at the time, the vegetarian restaurant) is God. No matter what we discover, what we learn, it is God appearing tangibly and visibly to us, *as us, as our awakening or unfolding* conscious awareness (consciousness) of the infinity of that which is.

Every moment of every day—no matter what we name the thoughts, things and activities which constitute our day—is *always* an act of *awakening* to, becoming *consciously aware* of, that which *is* because that which *is* is the only *is*.

The act of *awakening*—becoming *consciously aware*—is *itself* tangible and visible experience because no awareness is unembodied. Awareness is always embodied. There is no unmanifested or unembodied God, truth, awareness. God is fully manifest, fully embodied, infinitely so. The kingdom of God (the *only* kingdom) is *finished*. Therefore *awareness* is finished, complete, whole. "The place whereon you stand is holy [whole] ground."[1] The whole secret, therefore, is *awakening to* the finished kingdom of

[1] Exodus 3:5

is. And awakening is an act of *awareness*, an act of becoming *consciously aware* of that which is.

Therefore the next question is *What is God?* What is "All things were made through Him, and without Him nothing was made that was made"? What is "God saw every thing that he had made, and, behold, it was very good"?

Here's the answer—and the missing key for all those who attempt to awaken spiritually, and to evidence the treasures and freedom of heaven on earth, but struggle with their awakening:

> "God is Spirit: and they that worship him
> must worship him in spirit and in truth."[1]

CONTEMPLATION

Ponder deeply throughout this week—day and night, hour by hour—that God is *spirit;* truth is *spirit;* you and all are *spirit,* therefore infinite, incorporeal and omnipresent in body, form, amount, nature, character and condition.

Realize that it is *your individual pondering, contemplating, keeping your mind on God* that is the "taking root" of truth in being—the lesson of Jesus' Parable of the Sower.

No one, not even Jesus or Gautama, can do this for us. Only *we ourselves* can do it.

The more deeply you ponder this truth, the more deeply you explore it, 'work' it, 'chew' on it—and the more you allow the silence (after or interwoven with pondering) to be the *space* in which and through which truth springs forth, blossoms and becomes fruitage (becomes the "image and likeness" of itself as more *consciously* felt and known, experienced)— the more those blossoms become tangible and visible as your experience of one om-

[1] John 4:24

nipresent harmony; one experience of good, 'inner' and 'outer'; the actual experience of oneness and completeness as your life.

Know that I Am with you now and throughout your journey of awakening, and eternally beyond.

The light of silence bathes you, supports you, is you.

The gentle balm of truth surrounds you, protects you, and awakens your senses more so every moment.

TAKING THE FIRST TRUTH
DEEPER

As the roots of a plant grow, so do its young branches, buds, leaves and flowers. The 'inner' growth is evident as 'outer' form too. One without the other is impossible because the plant is *one whole organism* not 'two' separate parts; not 'one' feeding or producing a separate 'other' but *all* happening as *one* formation and activity. The more deeply and more developed the roots become, the greater and more abundant are the outer forms of foliage, buds, flowers and fruit—all *one* expression happening.

In this way, the more deeply truth is *known* and *felt* as true, and *as one*—the more truth is *lived* rather than occasionally thought about; the less we attempt to 'use' truth to improve our 'outer' experience of life; the more we are aware of the already-existent *oneness and completeness of truth* rather than accepting a false belief of an 'inner' versus 'outer' sense of life—*then* the more tangibly evident is the *whole* of our 'inner' *and* 'outer' harmony, consciously being lived as one harmonious and complete presence, one peaceful and fulfilled formation.

Miracles of truth begin to reveal themselves as we take the roots of truth deeper into the spiritually enriched soil of consciousness, just as the miracle of the vine reveals its multitude of buds, foliage, flowers and fruit as its roots continue to grow deeper and wider, nourished by rich and fertile soil.

It is, therefore, with such joy that we take the first truth deeper this week, remembering that just *one* truth statement contains the *whole* of truth, therefore the *whole* of the fruitage of truth.[1]

NOT 'WORK' BUT FULFILLMENT

Remember, what we are doing is not 'work'; it is the 'growth' (the revealing) of *your truth of being*—the miracle of the infinity of you and your world, your true fulfillment of being and purpose—tangibly evident, formed and real here and now.

Taking these truth statements deeper and deeper into your being (becoming ever more *aware* of truth) is not 'practice' for some future good. It is the actual revealing of the truth of you, the infinity of your being, evident here and now, this day, just as the growing roots of the vine are not 'practice' for next year's blossom and fruit, but are this season's fulfillment—the fulfillment of *now*.

Each day of root growth beneath the ground is 'also' revealed as greater foliage, blossom and fruit growth above the ground, *all being one whole*. It may seem for a short while, to material awareness, as if the roots grow 'before' more leaves and fruit appear. But the more we are aware of omnipresence—of *one whole* rather than 'two' separate parts—the *more immediately the fulfillment of oneness* is experienced. All already *is* because only God is, and all that God is and has already is, and forever is omnipresent. Nothing of God, spirit, truth—therefore nothing of anything anywhere, at any time, under any condition or for any reason—*becomes* truth, *becomes* manifest, *becomes* tangible, *becomes* visible. All *already and forever is*.

---

[1] See IN THE BEGINNING

REALIZATION OF THE FINISHED KINGDOM

Never let the truth of the finished kingdom slip from
your awareness. Keep it *alive* in your awareness each and
every moment:

*Only God is, therefore the only kingdom—the only mind, body,
world and universe, the only formation, the only experience—is
God. There is "none else"—no other kingdom, formation or experience. However, my* AWARENESS *of this truth determines how
much of truth I experience as my reality.*

*God is finished, whole and complete. Wouldn't it be ridiculous
to believe that God is unfinished and incomplete, still needed to
finish off his kingdom? Yes, of course God is finished and perfectly
so. Not a grain or single moment is incomplete, imperfect or unfulfilled. And because God is all, all is complete, perfect and fulfilled.*

*Wholeness, oneness, completeness—fulfillment—is the nature
of God, therefore the nature of mind, body, world and universe.
Nothing but God exists; nothing but the omnipresence, omnipotence and omniscience of God exists, therefore is the existence, the
presence and the formation of all.*

Indeed, God is whole and complete; God is utterly finished and fulfilled, whole, complete, perfect.

God is not still working on his kingdom. Nothing is
'born,' 'growing,' 'maturing,' then 'dying.' Nothing is
'evolving' in God, truth. The kingdom *is;* the universe *is;*
the earth *is*—all one finished body and organism of truth,
God, paradise, infinite in form, expression and purpose;
omnipresent as you, me, all.

The spiritual universe *is* before (meaning 'within,' not
'before' as in time) the universal *image* or *experience*.[1] Spiritual man is before the *image* of man (named 'mental and

within

[1] Genesis 1:1

physical'); light fills the universe before the *image* of the sun is in the sky.

God *is* mind *is* form; therefore we can understand the statements God is 'before' the form we call man, light is before the form of the sun, heaven is before the form of the earth. That which *is*, is an image and likeness of itself in or as experience—"the image and likeness of God."

All already is; everything we behold as formation—imagery—is 'secondary' experience, 'earthly' experience (that which is named 'human, material, physical' formation).

All is God's perfect spiritual kingdom, being, body, form, activity, amount from 'the beginning' (the very essence and substance). All is the omnipresence of infinity itself, *happening as you*. "I Am the Lord, and besides me there is none else."[1]

All is sublime being-ness in divine order, undisturbable bliss, peace, joy and purpose of being—immaculate beyond comprehension, transcendental, boundless, celestial, beatific, sacred, wondrous beyond—eternally beyond—the deepest possible intellectual experience.

GOD IS; AWARENESS MOVES

What appears to be born, to grow, develop, mature and eventually die is simply collective and individual *awareness moving*. God already is; the finished kingdom is what it suggests: *finished*. God is wholly finished. Omnipresence is wholly finished and present here and now *as* you, *as* me, *as* all—"The place whereon you stand [you are being] is Holy [whole; omnipresent] ground."[2] What appears as evolution, growth, development, progress is simply *awareness evolving*, not God evolving.

The critical truth to realize is that all is already whole,

[1] Isaiah 45:6   [2] Exodus 3:5; Acts 7:33

finished, in perfect divine completion and order. Nothing—not a grain or fiber or wisp or form or amount—is missing from you, separate or apart from you and your every moment of tangible experience, at every step, every breath, every point of you.

All is one, without exception, without condition, without process. You are that oneness; I am that oneness; all is that oneness—in its perfect finished state of being and experience—simply witnessed as 'happening' or 'evolving' or 'growing' *as an act of moving awareness* but never as an actual act, an act of God, because God does not act. God already *is*, that *is* being utterly whole and finished, done, complete and perfect. That which is already finished and perfect does not need to act and indeed does not.

It is because the finished kingdom of God—oneness, wholeness, omnipresence—is true that there is no 'practice' for some future good experience. All deepening of spiritual awareness *is itself* the *revealing* of more of the omnipresent good that is God as all. Every degree of truth realized *is itself* that degree of the infinity of being revealed and witnessed as real in experience.

As we know this truth—"Know the truth and that very truth will set you free"—we become less anxious and more restful. We have more peace and spaciousness about us. In confidence and joy we get on with the activity of deepening truth awareness by 'working' with these truth statements.

The *very act* of pondering truth more and more deeply, the very act of forever expounding and substantiating our individual awareness of the great spiritual truths *is the revealing* of greater and richer tangible forms and activities of good in our experience. Why is this true? God awareness *is* tangible experience. God or truth awareness does not *produce* good, healthy, abundant and harmonious form;

God awareness *is*, or *reveals* (not 'produces') its own formation—the image and likeness of God, good, truth. Just
as the very act of the roots of the vine growing and spread-
ing 'under the ground' *is* the growth and flourishing of the
vine's leaves, blossoms and fruit, so is the very act of knowing truth the revealed formation of itself as good and abundant earthly experience.

All is one happening: the oneness of omnipresence revealing ever more of itself to and as individual experience
*by the activity of becoming ever more consciously aware of the
finished kingdom of God as all.*

The grass of the world does not grow; awareness moves
as the specificity of the finished kingdom of 'grass' which
itself is forever whole, divine, perfect and untouchable.
Moving awareness appears as, therefore is experienced as,
grass growing, needing to be cut and manicured, then
growing again. No material activity ever touches or dis-
turbs (cuts) the true grass (divine idea beheld as form). It
ever *is* and remains a divine state of untouchable, un-dis-
turb-able, divine and perfect form, but experiential *awareness moving* within the sense of time and space makes it
seem to grow, be cut, grow again.

In the same way, you are forever whole and complete,
the divinity of being individually and uniquely *being the
whole* of the finished kingdom of God *happening as experience.* Here, now and forever, you and every minute detail
and activity of you and your entire world is whole and
complete—the finished kingdom of unconditional good
and harmony. All is one being, one happening, one form,
one experience, never 'two,' never God or God-awareness
producing or *manifesting* or eventually *becoming* produced,
manifested, demonstrated, tangible and visible experience. No, all *is*, and that *is* is perfectly and fully and already manifested, demonstrated, tangible and visible here

and now—which is all *oneness* can be.

So now, as we continue to delve more deeply into conscious awareness of the truth of being—*your* and every individual's truth of being—by our ever deeper pondering, contemplating, and meditating on these truths, we realize that this *very act is now* to be evident as greater, richer, more joyous, beautiful and harmonious tangible experience *as the oneness* of 'both' inner and outer experience.

Truth realization is never 'work' for some future 'result.' Never believe you are 'practicing' for some future good. Truth realization is the *here* and *now* of spiritual experience, purpose, being—'inner' and 'outer' all one. "Make the inner the outer, and make the outer the inner."[1]

Truth realization is the here and now of revealed freedom, infinity and omnipresence as all. It is infinity revealed as you, oneness revealed as you, wholeness and harmony revealed as you and everything of your world. It is heaven revealed as earth (you, me, all). "On earth as it is in heaven; I am the Lord, and besides me [God, spirit, truth, heaven] there is none else."

TAKING THE PROFOUND FIRST TRUTH MORE DEEPLY INTO CONSCIOUSNESS

Knowing what has been said today, let us gleefully and with joyous openness and expectation ponder, even more deeply, our First Truth of truths:

"All things were made through Him, and without Him nothing was made that was made."

"God saw every thing that he had made, and, behold, it was very good."

[1] *Gospel of Thomas*, Saying 22

"God is Spirit: and they that worship him must worship him in spirit and in truth."

More often and more deeply than ever before, *live* with this incredible truth morning noon and night—every hour of every morning, noon and night.

Observe every person, thing, amount, condition and place with the realization that no matter how it appears to be to 'human' awareness, no matter how it acts, its nature, its character, its form, color, scent, taste, its seeming reason or purpose, what every he, she or it *actually* and *literally is*, here and now in and as this very form being observed, is God, spirit and truth—the infinity and omnipresence of God appearing to be finite, omnipresence appearing to be locally present.

The only thing that ever presents itself to us is God. Everything observed is that which is "made through him, and without him nothing was made that was made." And because the 'he, she or it' of your awareness is God only and therefore *of* God only (of the oneness of God, omnipresence), 'he, she or it' is "very good" in truth—"God saw every thing that he had made, and, behold, it was very good."

Realize more deeply than ever before that every 'he, she or it' is spirit and truth—"God is spirit: and they that worship him must worship him [recognize all] in spirit and in truth."

BE SPACIOUS, STILL, OPEN, SILENT

In order to achieve this deeper awareness of truth we must slow down. We must have, *be*, a being of spaciousness, gentleness, stillness, peace, tranquility and receptivity. In this state of being the miracle of truth is evident.

In the normal hustle and bustle of 'human, material' activity, truth cannot possibly be evident. Whatever your state of being is—your overall belief, awareness or "ingredients" of being (primarily spiritual versus primarily material)—*is* what you experience as your world and the nature and character of all beings, things and conditions in your experience. The more you 'spiritualize' your being, the more of the good formation of spirit you experience as everything everywhere of your world.

The truthful state of being is *peaceful, still, spacious, receptive and lives with an air of silence about it.* Therefore, only in and as *that state of being* can truth be evident.

That makes sense, doesn't it?

If truth *is* spirit (which it is), and spirit is peace, stillness, spaciousness and silence, then it is understandable and logical that truth can only be experienced by spiritual being, which is a being of—at least a degree of—peace, stillness, spaciousness and living silence. The more spiritually peaceful, still and spacious you become, the more of peace, stillness and fulfillment you witness as your world because being and the forms of being—this world— are not separate, apart or different from each other, but are one.

Lastly, always remember that after, or interwoven with, your pondering, contemplating, meditating *have plenty of silence.* Be silence many, many times throughout the day if only for ten or twenty minute periods.

It is only in and as the *silence of being* that the revealing of greater *forever-present* truth formation is evident and tangible as experience.

"I AM" WITH YOU ALWAYS

You are never alone. You are one with the illumined consciousness of this message, one with the body of readership, one union of being, one gathering of being awakening to its truth. "Where two or more of you are gathered in my name, there am I among you."[1]

You are, each and every one, continually in my consciousness. I know you as the truth of being. You and your entire world is, this minute, the whole of God fully present and complete. I, Paul, do not have to 'personally' know that you are reading this book, and mentally keep you in 'my' consciousness. Consciousness knows. The one supreme and omnipresent consciousness *is* yours and mine, all one, and fully *aware* of its allness.

Therefore, rest and relax in my—the one—consciousness. It knows; it already is your allness and harmony, wholeness and freedom.

Your very conciousness, as you know this wondrous truth, supports and protects your entire experience, flooding you and every grain of your experience, permeating every nook and cranny, every place and condition with the visibility and tangibility of its presence, its formation, and its activity as your all-in-all.

As you know this and rest and relax, being open to it, you begin to *feel* truth's presence stirring and welling up within—filling you, being all that you are and have, revealing the life, love, beauty, bounty, harmony and peace that is the truth of all.

[1] Matthew 18:20

ILLUMINED UNDERSTANDING
OF THE FIRST TRUTH

✤

Perhaps the most wonderful and clarifying word we can use to understand what God is—what the truth, infinity and omnipresence of all is—is *consciousness.*

God is consciousness. Let us not believe we know this! Yes, we've heard it a thousand times but we *know it* only when we are experiencing it, being it—when we are witnessing the very presence and form of God, truth, limitlessness as our reliable, everyday experience 'within' and 'without'—only as we lose the 'fog' or 'veil' of material sense, material belief, material effort to reveal truthful being, body, form, activity, and amount.

So, with 'unknowing,' yet an eager and fertile receptivity, let us delve more deeply into consciousness being what God—therefore all—is. Without a clear and tangible understanding of God, we cannot experience truth *alive, real and practical* in our experience. In that case, truth would be of no value to us or the world, which of course is untrue.

God, truth, is the *one reality*—perfectly tangible and practical, and immediately so for those willing to sufficiently spiritualize their awareness.

GOD IS CONSCIOUSNESS

God is consciousness. The entirety of God—the entirety of the infinitude, all that God is and has, therefore all that is (because God is all)—is consciousness.

The *all* that we name *God*—which is one hundred percent consciousness—exists utterly complete, manifested, demonstrated, tangible and visible as the whole of itself in perfect, intricately divine order (oneness) at every point of itself simultaneously. There is no place or condition anywhere in infinity in which, or as which, this is untrue; in which God is lacking or not entirely visible and tangible, manifested and already demonstrated. If God *could* be lacking anywhere, under any circumstance, or be less than the whole of itself anywhere, or exist in an unmanifested or undemonstrated form in some places but not others, God would not be infinite and omnipresent but finite and partially present—not just finite and partial but *conditionally so.* Of course, the oneness and only-ness, the infinity and omnipresence that God is makes such a suggestion or belief nonsensical.

Realize here and now, God is *the* infinitude, *the* omnipresence, *the* oneness of all, there being "none else," therefore leaving none out or lacking in the fullness of God. The whole of God *is*—without there being any 'other' or 'different' *is*—which brings us to the truth that the fullness of God is unconditionally present and available to, and as, and for all. There is nothing other than God anywhere in the universe to which, or as which, God would have to 'become' available, or become 'more' available, or fully available. God *already is,* and that *is* is the only being, mind and formation, the only world and universe and everything everywhere of the world and universe. Everything everywhere is—despite belief and appearance—the unconditional, fully manifested presence of God, good.

The divine wholeness and order of all—consciousness—is itself the infinite and omnipresent body of awareness (experience), appearing to the five-sense and three-dimensional mind as individual you, me and all.

There is no life but the whole of life itself (God, oneness, eternity) being—in earthly experience—an infinity of individual beings, each unique and intricately perfect and purposeful bodies of awareness. Material awareness observes beings as 'physical,' but all being is spiritual and eternal for "there is none other." You are that, I am that, all is that.

The very fact that you are alive—that you *have life*—means that you are and have the only life there is, which is God-life, infinite life, eternal life.

You are the whole of life; the whole and intricately perfect being living its divine infinity, omnipresence and eternity. You are and have all the life that God is. You are the whole of God-life being the entirety of itself as you and all of your experience.

You are the one body of truth fully and vitally aware of its purposeful presence and form, its boundless spiritual faculties and resources. "Son, you are ever with me, and all that I have is yours. . . . [1] I am that I am. . . . [2] Your are the temple of the living God."[3]

GOD IS GOD ALONE—100 PERCENT PURE CONSCIOUSNESS

God is pure consciousness, there being—literally—none else. "I am the Lord, and besides me there is none else." It is by misunderstanding this truth—this fact—that spiritual identity, therefore *evidence*, falls down. Despite

over 4000 years of masterful and substantially demonstrated spiritual teaching, the majority still 'fail' in truth.
Why? Because there is belief in God—pure consciousness—*and* matter: a material, physical being and universe;
God (good, oneness) *and* cause and effect, time and space,
good and bad.

False understanding has us believing that we and our
world, and everything everywhere of it is not God but
matter, physicality, vegetable, animal and human, then attempting to 'save, transform, heal and prosper' that which
is believed to be incomplete and inharmonious—a life separate and different from God. Worst of all, we attempt to
go to God to have it done for us, as a special favor granted
because of our prayers or meditation or truth-thinking or
silence. "Ye ask, and receive not, because ye ask amiss."

Orthodox and much metaphysical teaching has left us
believing that God is some kind of spiritual storehouse
from which we can 'order' or draw or manifest our material good. We have been led to believe that God, pure consciousness, is somehow 'brought to' or 'converted to' the
'material, physical' experience of life to save, transform or
heal it.

It is this very belief that *is itself* the sense of separation
from that which we actually and already are and have (the
whole of God, the whole of infinity and omnipresence).
And because *belief is experience*, the *sense* of being separate
and different from God leaves us imprisoned in an experience devoid of God's (truth's) wholeness, completeness
and freedom of being.

The belief that something 'other' than the pure experience of God itself has to happen in order for 'material,
physical' life to be free and full of good is the very belief
that leaves experience devoid of *witnessed God*—unconditional good. God as mind as formation is fully and uncon-

ditionally present as all being, mind, body and experience. More than 'present,' God *seeks us,* forever beckoning our attention, our understanding and our trust. Indeed, we, our minds, bodies and world are filled to overflowing with God, good, and simply have to awaken to our truthful identity in order to experience God as formation. "The earth is full of the goodness of God." When we know (awaken) to this truth, that which *is*—our and our world's truth and freedom—becomes ever more tangible and real, and quickly so.

There is nothing but pure and omnipresent God, pure consciousness, but we have not awakened to this truth. Right here on this point is the reason so few, even of the spiritually fertile of the world, fail to experience the great treasures and promises of truth in and as every day life. It is the sole reason we struggle with life, in any and every particular way struggle and hardship are still experienced, individually and collectively. No other reason exists for the lacks, limitations, discords and diseases that rack and ravage our world. There is no place other than God, pure consciousness, to seek the solution to any and every problem the world—including each and every individual being—has or ever will have. The immediate solution to any problem lies already manifest, demonstrated and freely available in consciousness.

LIFE IS PURE CONSCIOUSNESS

Consciousness (life, God, spirit, truth) does not have within it or as it—nor does it produce or form or become or change into—a material, physical body, form, object, amount, condition, circumstance, or activity. Material belief believes it does or has, but this is entirely untrue. "Judge not by the appearance...."[1] I am the first, and I am the last,

[1] John 7:24   [2] Isaiah 44:6

and besides me there is no God [truth, actuality]."[2]

Pure consciousness does not change its nature, substance, body, form, amount or activity, nor *can* it, nor would it have a reason to. *I am the only; only I exist; I am all, therefore only I am 'needed.'*

Pure consciousness is all there is—the infinite itself, there being nothing else of existence possible. Otherwise the infinite would not truly be infinite, which of course is impossible. Therefore pure consciousness is the only truthful experience, the only experience which is full, whole, complete, perfect and free.

Living as pure consciousness is the only way in which the harmony and fullness, abundance and freedom, joy and purpose of life is experienced.

There is not God-life *and* your life, or mine. There is not God-life *and* converted God-life appearing as material, physical, human life. There is *only God-life*—oneness alive as the fullness of itself, being all that is.

THE PURITY OF CONSCIOUSNESS

God is not 'within' your mind or body. God is the 'withinness' of consciousness, which means the *purity* or *essence* of consciousness.

The term 'within consciousness' means *pure consciousness*, not any kind of physical withinness; not a center within a shell; not a central substance or beingness 'within' a body or a mind, but *pure consciousness* devoid of, or before thought, word, thing, name.

This is the great key to spiritual living: living the experience of pure consciousness without or before a thought, a word, a thing, a name.

The whole of infinity, the whole of God, the whole of everything the infinite is and has—all the infinity of mind, body, form, thing, activity, amount, condition, circumstance, place, world, universe—is pure consciousness. Nothing else exists; nothing else at all exists.

Therefore, if we believe the need or desire for anything 'else' *at all,* there is the reason for the experience of lack and limitation, disease and discord.

There is nothing 'other' than God itself, consciousness itself; therefore if we have a sense of anything 'else' or any condition or experience needed or desired other than pure God itself—pure consciousness itself—then the reason that we struggle along in lack and limitation becomes obvious.

ILLUMINED UNDERSTANDING
OF THE FIRST TRUTH

With this clarity, let us now gain a purer understanding of the First Truth:

All things were made through Him, and without Him nothing was made that was made.

God saw every thing that he had made, and, behold, it was very good.

God is Spirit: and they that worship him must worship him in spirit and in truth.

Let us interpret these three truths as—

All things were (are) made through and as pure consciousness, and without pure consciousness nothing was (is) made that was (is) made.

Pure consciousness sees every thing that it has made, and behold, it is very good—very pure, made of pure consciousness.

God is pure consciousness: and they that worship him must worship him in the truth—the undeviating fact—that all is pure consciousness.

THIS WEEK

Let us devote each hour of this week—as our 'formal' meditation and silence periods and as maintained underlying awareness during our work and family activities—to knowing that only pure consciousness is, that nothing at all exists but pure consciousness, and that, therefore, all we need and all we can desire is, and must be, only that of pure consciousness.

All 'else,' all appearance, is nothing more than the mind forming three-dimensional imagery of God, and sensing that which is nothing but God in five primary ways—seeing, hearing, tasting, touching and smelling. There is nothing 'else' about the whole of experience, *yet there appears to be*. But that which appears to be is nothing but experiential imagery—imaginations; conceptual mind forms of the one pure consciousness, the omnipresence and infinity of all, forever unchanged and unchangeable God. "I live, and move, and have my being in God."

Stay consciously aware of this truth every hour as best you can. Then have as much 'formal' meditation on it—pondering it, deepening your awareness of it, opening out the truth of it as your reality and the reality of all—as you can each day.

Also realize this, and allow yourself to experience it as often as you can each day: God, consciousness, is *silence*.

The infinity of good, omnipresent right where you are, happening as the truth and wholeness of you, the boundless and omnipresent completeness of you this and every minute of your experience, is only found to tangibly be, and only visibly experienced in and as and 'through' *silence.*

Therefore, only as we are silent—attentive, keen and responsive to the infinity of pure consciousness happening as the truth of individual being, the individual, unique and intricately perfect and whole in every detail *you* that you are—do we discover the solution to every individual and collective problem, no matter what that problem is, or how urgent, overwhelming, large-scale or impossible to overcome it seems to be to human awareness.

Not only do we discover the solution 'within' and as silence—pure consciousness—but we discover it to be already manifest, whole, complete and perfect to all involved. "Before you call I will answer." Before the naming of anything, before the conceptual experience, before any 'human' or 'worldly' experience—either good or bad—God *is forever the manifested truth of all;* pure consciousness *is forever the manifested truth of all;* perfection *is forever the manifested truth of all;* therefore, in and as God, in and as pure consciousness, harmony is discovered, fully and freely available as practical experience. Before, before, before! Within, within, within!

Do you see this now? Do you see where confusion has lived, therefore how experience has continued, by degree, to lack God, to be limited, discordant, disharmonious, diseased and in poverty, and why we have been unable to free ourselves of it?

Live with this message over and over until the undeviating truth of it strongly registers in your awareness. Meditate on it ceaselessly; let silence be your way of living, your way of experience, never again allowing world belief to convince you there is something 'else' you or the world needs. There is nothing else you need because nothing 'else' exists. Pure consciousness is all there is. Live as and on it. Feast on it. Love it alone, seek it alone, be the body of awareness whose reality is pure consciousness alone.

Realize truth; let truth live you in and through your daily periods of *silence*. Then watch the daily miracle that takes place as your experience.

WEEKS FOUR – NINE

THE
SECOND
TRUTH

THE SECOND TRUTH

❖

Do you now thoroughly see and understand that God—spirit and truth—is infinite and omnipresent, that, therefore, nothing exists, despite the way it appears to be or act, *but* God?

Do you see that *all* is God, period? Do you see that there is not, and cannot ever be, an exception to this wondrous truth? Has it registered within you that nothing in the whole of the infinitude has power or even influence over God, to somehow 'change' that which is one hundred percent God—the *only* presence and power—into something less or different or temporal? Do you hear the logic of truth as it whispers, How could God which is incorporeal, infinite, omnipresent, omniscient and omnipotent be changed by some 'greater' or even 'equal' power into corporeality, finiteness, local presence, human intelligence, or personal, objective power? What would that 'greater' or 'equal' power be when God is the *only*? Where would it exist when God is the *only* existence, the only place—and the omnipresence of all existence and place?

The infinitude—God—is what the word suggests, *infinite*. It is for this reason that nothing but infinity can exist and indeed does not; nothing but oneness, spirit and truth, exists. Nothing 'else' exists because there isn't anything 'else' that could exist—no other substance, presence, life or formation that could exist. *Only God is.*

Therefore, if anything at all exists—anything and everything within and throughout all of infinity and eternity, whether 'we' (material, finite, objective sense and belief) name it a person, animal, plant or vegetable, object, amount, activity, place, condition or circumstance—that existence, without exception, is God, spirit and truth.

The only thing that exists is God; the only thing that can ever present itself to you is God, for there is—most literally—none else.

Furthermore, because the whole of God exists at every point of itself at the same time—omnipresence being omnipresent—anything and everything that exists, without exception, is the *whole* of God, the *whole* of spirit and truth, simply *appearing to be* (to sense) a particular 'he, she, it, activity, amount, place, condition or circumstance.'

Appearance—as long as we believe its face value, believe it to be something in and of its own self—is one hundred percent deceptive. Spirit and truth have *nothing* to do with the way in which God appears conceptually *if that appearance is believed to be an actual entity in and of its own self.*

The way spirit and truth appear to be as observed through, and experienced as, the five 'human' senses and three dimensions of mind has nothing whatsoever to do with what is truthfully present here, there and everywhere, what truth actually is as form. Yet, when everything of experience is truly known to be God and not just what it appears to be—then all of formation becomes illumined and revealed as whole, harmonious, healthy, boundless, loving, peaceful and purposeful.

Do you thoroughly understand this now? So much so that you can observe anything of experience and not be fooled by its appearance, but know—*really know*—that it is the very presence of God itself, therefore infinity, omnipresence, omniscience and omnipotence itself, *incorporeal presence*, there being none else?

If so, then you are ready for the Second Truth to be planted in the soil of awareness. If not, devote yourself longer to reading about and meditating with the truth we've been given to this point—the truth of *God being all*—until it alights with you and becomes strong and firm as that which you *know*, not just hope for.

THE EARTH

The earth is the Lord's and the fullness thereof.

This is the great key to oneness *experienced tangibly* both 'in' and 'out.' The 'earth'—which is unfortunately believed to be of matter (material and physical; corporeal)—is simply an earthly *sense* of spirit, a corporeal *sense* of that which is one hundred percent incorporeal. The earth and everything everywhere in it and of it is nothing less than or different from the *fullness (omnipresence) of God.*

Why is that true? Because God is infinite; *the infinitude itself* being the experience of itself at our degree of awareness—the degree we call 'human.' God *is* the earth, the universe and infinitely beyond, and everything in it and of it. God is not 'within' the earth or 'within' being somewhere, or 'within' the universe; God *is* the earth, universe and all because God *is all.* The notion of 'inner' versus 'outer' does not exist in God, omnipresence; therefore it does exist anywhere. There is *only* and *all*—omnipresent—God. The notion of matter or corporeality does not exist in God, therefore does not exist at all. Matter—corporeality—is nothing but a *sense* of that which is the infinite ocean of spirit or incorporeality. That sense in and of its own self is innocent. Remember this. There is nothing wrong or untrue about sense itself. It is only if or when we introduce *belief* to sense, that whatever is being sensed becomes *in experience* (never in truth) the nature and quality of the particular belief being entertained.

Realize now, and meditate upon these truths:

All *experience* is God, and is *of* God. What 'else' could experience be or consist of if all is God—which, indeed, all is?

All *being* is God. What 'else' could being be or consist of if all is God?

All *body, organ and function* is God. What 'else' could body, organ and function be or consist of if all is God?

All *thing* is God. What 'else' could anything be or consist of if all is God?

All *amount* is God. What 'else' could amount be or consist of if all is God?

All *activity* is God. What 'else' could activity be or consist of if all is God?

All *place* is God. What 'else' could place be or consist of if all is God?

All *condition and circumstance* is God. What 'else' could condition and circumstance be or consist of if all is God?

BUT...

The way *all* is experienced through and as the human

five senses and three dimensions in and of its own self is illusion, maya, misconception—a foggy or dim, slow (very slow) faculty of *awareness*.

There is *no truth* in what appears to be—the way God *appears to look and act* through, or to, the five senses if he, she or it is believed to be an entity in and of its own self. Just as we can say that there is no truth to the *appearance* of the sun 'turning itself off' at dusk, we can say that by appearance alone we cannot and do not evidence God, truth. The sun does not turn itself off at dusk even though it appears to. The sun shines just as brightly as it always does, but the *appearance* of dusk to human sense looks as if the sun is dimming. Appearance at its face value is deceptive whether we're talking of the sun or God—in fact, of anyone or anything!

No matter what appears as everything everywhere materially and physically—good or bad, positive or negative, much or little, ease or struggle, peace or war, harmony or disharmony—there is *no truth to that appearance.*

Lao Tzu's eye-opening statement, "If you can name it, it is not true" is *literal.* Only God is. The first truth—its three statements—have given us a beautiful clarity about only God is; only spirit and truth is; only infinity, omnipresence, omniscience, omnipotence is, only *incorporeality* is.

Now we can easily understand why *The earth is the Lord's and the fullness thereof.*

No matter what we 'name God' (the infinitude of being and experience)—in this case the name 'earth'—it is still and only God, for there is literally, and in the most practical way, "none else."

OUR WORK THIS WEEK

Devote yourself this week to pondering, more and more consistently and deeply, at every moment, the truth that everything everywhere of experience, everything that touches your awareness—every being, object, animal, insect, plant, vegetable, activity, amount, condition, circumstance and place, *everything* you see, hear, taste, touch, smell and think about—is, in fact and despite appearance, "the earth" that is "the Lord's and the fullness [omnipresence] thereof."

Realize that the *appearance* of *all* in your life, without exception—despite the way it *appears to be* and *act*, despite its apparent nature, character, form, size, weight, amount; despite its name—is in truth, *God, infinity itself* and the *whole of infinity* simply appearing through, or to, any one or all of your five senses to be the finite and local 'he, she or it' you're experiencing.

Simply stated: everything everywhere is God, infinity, truth, spirit, omnipresence despite the way it appears.

Remember, *depth* of spiritual awareness is the key to lifting and enriching experience, just as the depth of the tree's roots is the key to its size and magnificent foliage and fruitage. Evidencing truthful experience is *all* about *depth* of spiritual awareness, a depth that transforms awareness to certainty.

Therefore, the *more deeply* you ponder this truth—the more *earnestly* you contemplate the truth of everything that comes into or up against your awareness hour-by-hour, day-by-day, and the more *consistently* you flame your awareness that *God is the only* despite the way everything of the material, physical, worldly experience *seems and looks to be*—the more you are spiritually lifting and enriching your awareness of truth.

And the more you lift and enrich—*spiritualize*—your awareness, the more of spiritual harmony, life, abundance, peace, joy, love and fulfillment of purpose you tangibly experience. Remember, awareness is experience. There is no 'unembodied' or 'unmanifested' or 'undemonstrated' God, therefore God *awareness* (the conviction of God being all).

THE REVELATION OF ONENESS

❧

I f *the earth is the Lord's and the fullness thereof,* then *all* not
only *is* God, spirit and truth, but also 'belongs' to God,
spirit, truth. All is God—all, all, *all*—therefore all is God's.

All is God *being* allness; all is the macro *being* the micro,
the micro *being* the macro—indubitable omnipresence,
oneness. All is God *being* the fullness of itself, the completeness of itself, the oneness of itself, the harmony,
peace, bliss of itself alone. All is oneness *as itself alone,* there
being none else, not even one other grain, atom or sub-
atomic particle existent in the whole of the infinitude, but
all one and one*ness*—self-complete, self-abundant, self-fulfilled at each and every point of itself at the same time.
Therefore, the presence and formation of all, and the
'ownership' and 'responsibility' of all, are God's and
God's alone.

All of experience is perpetually and invariably whole,
complete, in divine order and balance, under divine government, perfect, fulfilled, flawless and indefectible *because only God is,* which means that God is *all—all,* without
exception.

All is the *whole*—the omnipresence of infinity, om-
nipres*ent* as each specific moment, aspect and place of
awareness. Each specific moment and aspect of awareness—to dim 'human' sense—looks as if it is, or appears as
if it is *material or physical.* Appearance is described as

"earth" in this truth statement. "Earth" in scripture means *experience.*

It appears as if we are looking at—observing, experiencing—a particular and independent entity: an object, type of material, amount, size, weight, place, condition, distance or activity; a human being, animal, insect, plant, flower, color, fragrance, vegetable; a building, our home and neighborhood, our work, money, a forest, mountain, ocean, lake or river; a mineral, cell, atom or sub-atomic particle. It appears as if we are under the law or state of cause and effect, evolution, a multitude of conditions and consequences, belief, thought and effort, all existing in time and occupying particular places in space. Everything of life, it seems, is a consequence or result of something else. Everything seems to depend on a process and to take time to evolve or become the consequence or result of its cause. Experience seems to be full of good *and* bad, benefit *and* hindrance, asset *and* detriment, plus *and* minus.

It seems as if we can 'speed up' or 'slow down' life by our degree of knowledge and skill, how adept we become at increasing and maintaining the 'good' while decreasing or overcoming the 'bad.'

It seems as if we are subject to either positive or negative 'outside' forces or laws, forces or laws which are 'greater than we.' They work either for or against us. Some are constructive, some destructive. It seems as if it is down to 'luck' or 'destiny' or 'karma' as to which 'type' of force works for or against us, and in which department of life.

It seems as if we can 'improve' or 'heal' or 'succeed' or 'prosper' or 'save' or 'pacify' our experience if we have sufficient knowledge and skill, sufficient resource, sufficient numbers of the right friends or contacts—either of our own, or those of somebody else which we can borrow but then pay back, usually with interest. The 'force of health' works 'for us' while the 'force of disease' works 'against us.' The 'force of economics' combined with our individual 'knowledge and ability to be successful' in our chosen field either helps or hinders our success, security and prosperity in job, career, business or practice. Our 'ability in love' results in either true and lasting relationships, particularly our one, true love, or a string of unsatisfactory attempts at love, without finding or being able to 'keep' our one, true love. Our 'ability to uphold peace and harmony' as a human race determines the stability or instability of our family, business, neighborhood, state, country or world. It seems as if world peace, union, balance, love, equality, safety and security is 'controlled' by, therefore 'dependent' on, both individual and group intention, morality, decency, honesty, integrity.

We could carry on throughout every gamut of experience, but the truth is this: the way all *appears to be* is not the way all *is.*

ONLY GOD IS

Only God is, despite the way all appears to be to or as or through dim 'human' sense. *Only spirit and truth is,* despite the admittedly convincing way spirit appears to be matter in experience and truth appears to be good and bad in experience. Only God, spirit, truth is despite the dim or foggy *sense* of mind, body and world we believe and entertain—inclusive of all the apparent 'powers' of these and how they appear to act upon our experience, either for our benefit or our impediment. We heard in *Stand on Truth,* "Wherever you look, there *I am;* wherever you place your awareness, there *I am;* whatever you see, hear, taste, touch, smell or think, it is *I.*"

Yes, the earth is the Lord's and the fullness thereof.

WHATEVER IS, IS INFINITE
AND OMNIPRESENT

Because all is God, all is infinite and omnipresent. There are no 'numbers, measurement or quantity' in God; therefore there cannot be, and are not numbers, measurements or quantities in truthful experience. All, without exception (because there is no exception to the presence and wholeness of God as all), is infinity and omnipresence being experienced, simply *objectively*. But that objective experience does not, nor ever can *change* God. Nothing can change God; there is no other or separate or different power that could change God one iota. Indeed, God is the only, therefore the only presence and power, with nothing 'else' to influence or change it.

In this way, realize that the infinity and omnipresence of all is readily experience-*able* by any person living in truth. Truth, truthful experience, is not dispensed to only the holy or sufficiently prayerful or meditative few. No! What nonsense such a belief would be! God is *one, universal, all, unconditioned,* and unconditionally present and *available* as the reality of experience to and as and for all.

The greatest saint the world has ever seen has no more truth available to him or her than the greatest sinner, the greatest sinner no less truth available.

Never is truth personal, local, or available only as a special dispensation or favor from God to any one individual—not even to a Jesus or Gautama:

> I of my own self am nothing; . . .[1] The Father within me, he does these works. . . .[2] My Father and your Father [the one truth of all]. . . .[3] The works you see me do, you can do also, and greater than these you can do. . . .[4] God's rain falls equally on the just and

[1] John 5:30   [2] Isaiah 44:6   [3] John 20:17   [4] John 14:12

the unjust.[1]

There is no unmanifested or undemonstrated, invisible or intangible God. God is all, therefore is the only *is*, the only presence and the only formation. Whatever *is*, is infinity and omnipresence itself being that which is, that being God—the *only* existence. That which is being experienced at every successive moment, no matter whether a 'he, she, it, place, activity or amount' is infinity and omnipresence itself. God is the infinity of manifested and perfectly visible formation. Everything everywhere, ad-infinitum, is infinity itself being the very presence of itself as boundless and inexhaustible formation (mind, body, world, universe).

You are the infinity and omnipresence of being living in and as the freely available infinitude of experience. Everything everywhere—whether we name it person, place, thing, condition, plant, vegetable, mineral, cell, atom or subatomic particle—is infinity and omnipresence *being*, in experience, that being, that form, that condition, that activity or amount.

"The earth is the Lord's and the fullness thereof."

WHATEVER IS, IS IMPERSONAL

Because all is God, there is no personal self, nor personal thing. You are impersonal being, not personal being. You are the infinity of being and experience, not a finite being with finite experience.

You are the infinity of being with infinity as your resource, which never depletes, nor is ever *able* to deplete. Your world of resource is infinite, omnipresent and impersonal, one as all, for all, and to be shared unconditionally with all.

[1] Matthew 5:45

Because "The earth is the Lord's and the fullness thereof," you do not own anything—not even your mind, your body—not even a single breath or step. All is God and God's. You do not own any 'thing' or 'amount' anymore than you own sunshine, gravity, aerodynamics, mathematics, music, the ocean, sky, clouds, rain or snowflakes. All is God; therefore all is 'owned by' God and is universal, impersonal, infinite and unconditionally omnipresent, and freely available in experience.

YOU EXPERIENCE, NOT OWN

You *experience*. You do not *own*.

You individually, and we collectively, *experience* sunshine, gravity, aerodynamics, mathematics, music, the ocean, the sky, clouds, rain and snowflakes. You and we do not *own* these, not even one, or for one moment.

In the same way, because "The [whole] earth is the Lord's and the fullness [everything everywhere, without exception] thereof," you *individually experience* everything of life, but you 'own' nothing.

You are the guest of life, not the owner. You are the guest of *absolutely everything* of life, never the owner of a single thing. You are the guest of your body; you do not own it. You are the guest of your love relationship; you do not own him or her. You are the guest of your home, your furniture and furnishings, your electronics, your objects of art and play; you do not own them. You are the guest of money; you do not own it, nor can you earn it. You are the guest of your job, career, business or practice; you do not own it. You are the guest of your customers, clients, patients or students; you do not own them.

You are the guest of absolutely every person, thing, place, condition and activity in your universe. You own nothing because "The earth is the *Lord's* [not yours or mine] and the fullness thereof."

FREE THE EARTH,
THEN YOU *HAVE* FREEDOM OF ALL

In understanding the truth that all is God, therefore 'owned by' God, and in understanding that the whole of God is embodied in and as your individual consciousness because consciousness is indivisible and omnipresent— the *whole* of God present at and as each point of itself at the same time—you realize that "The earth is the Lord's and the fullness thereof" is true of *your very consciousness.*

You are that. "I am that I am." Your *unconditioned mind* is "the Lord"; therefore, "the earth and the fullness thereof" is yours—as unconditioned consciousness, God consciousness.

In releasing your sense of ownership of person, home, job, career, business, things, conditions, amounts, circumstances—everything of the personal sense of being—you free yourself as spiritual being. Imagine!—free of all ownership, therefore free of all bind and responsibility. The moment we free ourselves of the sense of ownership *in truth,* we free ourselves of all limiting, lacking, discordant and burdensome experience.

Every person, thing, amount or condition that has seemed to keep us bound, now cannot. We are free in spirit. We are *being* our freedom. We no longer attach to the conceptual experience in and of its own self—the physical 'persons' or material 'things, amounts and conditions' of experience. We stay unattached. We stay spacious, loose and free in God. We know that *in spirit,* in truth, we *are the very infinity and freedom of being itself.* We need nothing 'else' because *all is already us and ours.* "Son, you are ever with me, and all that I have is yours."[1]

I need nothing because I already am all. I *am* all. I *have* all. I am the infinity of consciousness, fully manifested and already demonstrated. I am infinite and omnipresent manifestation, infinite and omnipresent form, infinite and omnipresent being in every way—free, purposeful, omniscient and omnipotent, already and perpetually fulfilled. I *am* that I am—not because of my own truth or ability, but because "I can of my own self do nothing. . . .[2] the Father that dwells in me [as the whole of the 'me' I am] he does [is] the works [is the one presence, power and formation]."[3]

OUR WORK THIS WEEK

Ponder deeply, "The earth is the Lord's and the fullness thereof."

Ponder deeply that you own nothing, that all is God and God's, that all is impersonal, universal, "one for all, and all for one."

Start to detach from all you sense as being 'yours.' Start loosening and releasing your hold on all people, things, amounts, conditions, activities. Realize *all* as God and God's, not to be 'gained' or 'owned,' but humbly experienced and creatively and impartially shared as fulfillment of all being, of all of life, each hour and step of unfolding experience.

Start establishing a sense of true spaciousness about, and around, and as *all*—a deep stillness and spaciousness of you as the very being of truth, of spirit, of peace, of unconditioned consciousness.

Realize more and more deeply that as you release the beings, things and conditions of 'this world,' you are free in spirit. Then you *have all* in and as the infinity and free-

---

[1] Luke 15:31   [2] John 5:10   [3] John 14:10

dom of truthful experience.

In 'ownership' you are restricted, bound, limited to that which you 'own' and your belief about him, her or it. In releasing ownership—"whatever you loose on earth"[1]— you discover you *have* infinity and omnipresence, you *are* infinity and omnipresence, you *have* and *are itself* the substance, nature, character, form, activity and amount of infinity and omnipresence, unconditional and unbounded.

It is in releasing ownership—that of the personal sense of life—that you free yourself and discover your experience filled with all that God is and has—*all* at every moment, *all* as every here and now.

You are then the being and freedom of *spirit experiencing its infinity and omnipresence, its purpose and gift.* You are free in God as earth, with everything of God as your earthly mind, body, function and resource—all of God being one and omnipresent as every moment, place and condition of experience, "on earth as it is in heaven."

"I am in the world but not of it." I have the freedom of the world and everything it has *because* I know the truth— the truth that all is God, the truth that "The earth is the Lord's and the fullness thereof" and the truth that "I am that" because I and all cannot be anything other than the only *I* that exists.

"I am in the world but not of it." I am not of the world of humanity, objectivity, of concept, of matter, of cause and effect, of time and space, but of *truth.* I am *in* and having a conceptual, three-dimensional and five-sensed *experience* called 'this world,' but I am not *of* it. I realize that the three-dimensional, five-sensed experience—the world of formation, the world of God-*as*-mind-*as*-formation—is *in and of its own self innocent.* It contains neither good nor bad. It simply is. It is simply God experience (because there is no 'other' experience to have), and there never is

[1] Matthew 16:19

anything wrong or untruthful or un-God-like about experience—*unless we make it so* (unless we add *belief* to it).

I am not the being of belief but of truth, of God. I am the being of infinity and omnipresence; therefore I *am* and *have* infinity and omnipresence of all, without attaching to or owning a single thing or aspect or amount of my experience.

I am free in non-ownership, in the impersonal, universal, incorporeal truth of being, sharing all with all, unconditionally, impartially, each hour, each day.

The more I know my oneness of being and the more of it I *share*, the more I *have* as individual experience because as it 'pours out of me,' it becomes visible to my conceptual sense. The more of the impersonal, universal being of truth I am *being*, the more of the beauty, bounty, freedom and reality of infinity and omnipresence is my experience. "Give and it shall be given unto you, pressed down, shaken together, running over shall men [the whole material sense of experience] give unto you."

Think deeply on these things this week. Do not allow an hour to slip by you without turning your awareness to these astonishing truths—the truths of *you* and your world—*living* them ever more, and ever more *deeply* and *thoroughly*, realizing that the more deeply you know and live them, the more you make yourself a "window of heaven" which evidences truth as the one reality.

Lastly and always, give yourself the greatest gift of all, the gift of *silence*. Have many periods of silence each day, some short, some longer, and perhaps one long period of an hour or two, or longer, letting truth be *felt happening* within you, as you, and spilling out of you into and as your whole universe. Silence is the tangible experience of all that God is, in experience. God *is* silence; silence *felt happening* is God fully manifested, demonstrated, visible and tangible in experience. Silence is the greatest experience and the greatest gift.

Remember, as you *deepen* your awareness of these God-filled truths—by contemplating them, living with them, chewing on them, loving them—your awareness is enriched, and because awareness *is* experience, so is your palpable experience enriched.

I am with you 24 hours a day.

Stillness, peace and silence is yours.

Truth consciousness fills you, is you, and embraces you, supports you, lifts you, enriches you. Bathe in it many times throughout the day and night. Allow it to 'seek you' as you rest in its stillness, peace and completeness of being.

Stay receptive to the miracle of truth happening as you and as all of your experience.

THE LOST BUDDHA AND
CHRIST CONSCIOUSNESS

There is a sublime state of being that sees through all appearance to truth. It has been referred to as the *healing consciousness*. More accurately stated, it is the *revealing* consciousness—the consciousness that reveals or exposes truth where, to material awareness, untruth seems to exist.

It is the Buddha or Christ consciousness, that state of being that reveals, through the fog of 'human,' material belief, the infinity and omnipresence of God as all—the unchanging wholeness and perfection of all, the spiritual kingdom, the truth of all which forever and harmoniously *is*. Once attained, even by a true grain, the Buddha or Christ consciousness is able to reveal what to human perception is miracle after miracle of good.

Disease, discord, lack and limitation of any name or nature do not and cannot exist in the presence of this state of consciousness. Nothing but the tangible revelation of God—good without opposite—is possible to it and witnessed by it. It is now time for you to attain it.

NO 'GOOD' VERSUS 'BAD'

In the statement "The earth is the Lord's and the fullness thereof," we are given the truth of one presence. As always we must understand this statement as being literal. One presence—oneness itself, there being none other—is the literal truth and the one reality.

God *is*. Because God is the infinitude itself, omnipresent at and as each point of itself at the same time, it is clear that nothing 'else' other than the omnipresence of infinity *is*, or can be. Nothing 'else' exists and nothing 'else' can exist.

Strangely, 'human' logic learns that God *is*—that God is infinite, there being, therefore, nothing 'else'—then continues accepting the human self and material world with its pairs of opposites, all its lacks, limitations, discords and diseases, and the continued attempt to apply or bring God to its lacking-God experience.

In other words, only-God-is is not taken literally. "The earth is the Lord's and the fullness thereof" is not taken literally. If it were, every person who has grasped even a grain of its truth would be stopped in his or her tracks at every step, re-remembering and re-realizing that despite the way experience seems to be at any moment (what it seems to consist of, good or bad), all is actually God, therefore whole, harmonious, abundant and perfect. "Judge not according to the appearance, but judge righteous judgment."

Let us, therefore, deepen our understanding. The earth—even though every being and every thing of it appears conceptual, finite, separate, of many different natures, amounts, characters, categories and powers, many good and many bad—is actually and exclusively God and the fullness (omnipresence) of God. "The earth is full of the goodness of God."

When we are able to look at any being, thing, amount, place or condition—either of good or bad—and realize that despite the way it appears to be, it is actually, literally, and exclusively God, then we are attaining the God, Buddha or Christ consciousness.

ONLY GOD IS, THEREFORE ONLY ONE NATURE, QUALITY AND CONDITION IS

We have to observe all of experience and realize that despite the way it appears to be—its *seemingly real* nature, quality and condition, and its seeming effect on the rest of experience, either good or bad, constructive or destructive—*actually* and *truthfully* (which means actually and truthfully here and now, as the very form of experience you are observing) it is God, because only God is; therefore only one nature, quality and condition is: God, divine and omnipresent good.

The appearing he, she, it, place, activity, amount, circumstance or condition has no nature, quality or condition at all *in and of its own self.* "The earth is the Lord's and the fullness thereof." There is nothing but God (incorporeality, infinity and omnipresence) despite all and every apparent presence and experience—apparent reality.

When we can dismiss all apparent reality (appearance) in the realization of only-God-is—therefore the only nature, quality and condition *all is* and *all has* is God—we are able to 'invite' God, invite the one true reality, to be clear and manifest as our experience by opening our awareness to the *oneness* it is, the one reality of all, the one, true, already and forever *is.* How?

> "Be still [still the senses, making of your sense of self and experience a nothingness], and know that I am God. . . .[1] Stand still and see the salvation [harmony and wholeness] of the Lord [of truth, of *is*], which will be shown to you this day."[2]

[1] Psalm 46:10   [2] Exodus 14:3

Our truthful, untroubled, detached (from appearance), peaceful and receptive consciousness is the silence and openness which reveals truth where untruth seemed to be.

Only truth is. Only one (God) and one*ness* (God experience) is—one life, one being, one body, one presence, one power, one intelligence, one nature, one quality and one condition. It is only *belief* and the troubled, attached-to-appearance, separated-from-God *sense* that obscures truthful experience.

Truth stands all around you this minute, filling your very world with good, completeness and harmony. The world is the God-world, the only world in existence—oneness and omnipresence, "earth as it is in heaven." Indeed, "I live and move and have my being in and as God." We are forever witnessing God as formation (world) because only God is; therefore no 'other' formation could be witnessed. However, by believing that we and our world are something different from, or less than, God itself and by our attaching to appearance, believing it to be something in and of its own self—either loving, hating, or fearing the believed entities of experience—our senses are so foggy or dimly lit that we cannot see that which *is*.

Experiencing truth is all about seeing clearly. "Open his eyes that he may see."[1]

ACCEPT APPEARANCE AS 'JUST IS'

Appearance—experience—just *is*. It is just a multitude of pictures or formations. We don't have to understand it of its own self, make effort for or maintain its good, battle or attempt to overcome its bad, improve it, prosper it, pacify or heal it. *We don't even have to bring God to it.* God already *is* long, long before 'we' and 'our belief' arrive on

[1] 2 Kings 6:17

the scene. Hear it again: *I live and move and have my being in and as God.* Well, if that is true, which it is, why would I have to bring God to the world (appearance or experience)? Indeed, I do not—God already is all and is omnipresent as all. If I believe I *do* need to, or even *can*, I haven't yet awakened to the truth that only God is, that God *already* is, and that I of my own self am nothing, therefore unable to 'bring God to experience' even if it needed it, which it doesn't. The only thing needed is *my awakening* to the truth that *is* and that surrounds me as far as my senses can sense, within and without, infinite and omnipresent as and *being* all.

God is already present as this and every moment of experience, everywhere equally present, *being* all. There is nothing real in or of appearance as it seems to be, therefore nothing real with which to engage, or 'do' something about, maintain, fix or heal in and of its own self. It is appearance (formation) only. As far as it of its own self goes, it is, and has, nothing—no substance, no body, no power, no intelligence, no ability, no cause, no function.

That being so, why be either enamored with it or fearful of it, argue with it, battle with it, attempt to heal, pacify or prosper it, make it good? It *is God, only* God and *fully* God. It is just our material (false) *sense* of God that finitizes sensed experience, makes it seemingly consist of two powers, qualities and conditions (good and bad) instead of the *one* (God) it truly is.

This very misunderstanding of experience—along with the ongoing attempt to pacify, harmonize and heal that which has been misunderstood—has been the ineffectiveness and impracticality (in human experience) of the greatest spiritual teachings of the ages. Appearance 'just is.' Appearance *in and of its own self* does not matter. It has no reality, no power, no quality, no truth. Leave it alone and be unattached to it in the realization that only God is. Then in your relaxed, rested, quiet, untroubled and detached sense—because it has only ever been your unrested, busy, troubled and attached sense that obscures truth—the truth that stands all around you in its glorious formation becomes visible and tangible. The fog or 'darkness' of material belief dissolves to reveal the world of truthful form.

MISPERCEPTION

Let's say you are looking at railway tracks. From where you stand the tracks appear to be set at the accurate distance from each other. But up in the distance they appear to be joined together. How is that so? Are they truly joined together? No. What you are observing is nothing but an optical illusion. The appearance 'just is.' You cannot and do not need to deny the *appearance*. It is definitely 'happening' in this moment of your experience, but *what* is it? Is it real? Should you be concerned and do something about it? No, it is just an 'is' of experience, with nothing either good or bad about that 'is.'

You don't have to understand it of its own self, nor do you have to do anything about it. You don't have to run up there and force the tracks apart before the train arrives. You simply have to know the truth that, despite appearance, the tracks are perfectly set apart. "Know the truth, and that very truth will set you [and keep you] free."

Now let's say someone calls you with a headache. What will you do? Well, most so-called 'spiritual' practitioners will quickly get to work on either knowing the truth of the person, or the non-truth of the headache. What they have failed to realize—and are therefore unable to demonstrate—is that there is neither truth of the person as she or he appears, nor non-truth of the headache as it appears. The 'good' person is not *in truth* having a 'bad' experience. *Both* the 'good' and the 'bad' are just appearance, just an 'is' of experience. There is no truth or untruth to be found in either the appearance of the person or the headache.

Nothing of appearance (experience) in and of its own self is truth, nor can it of its own self evidence truth. Everything of appearance is just that: appearance, imagery, just an 'is' and nothing more, nothing different, nothing less. Because it is nothing but appearance, it of its own self does not consist of the pairs of opposites despite its suggestion of being 'good' or 'bad,' 'positive' or 'negative,' 'harmonious and complete' or 'disharmonious and incomplete.' The pairs of opposites are beliefs alone and do not, nor can, exist 'in' or 'of' that which is nothing but imagery. The imagery is innocent and acts so *when devoid of belief about it.*

NOTHING TO 'OVERCOME'

The saddest thing to witness these days in once- truthful spiritual teachings is the acceptance of appearance as something real, an entity in and of its own self, which truth, it is believed, can get rid of or 'heal'; and the acceptance of two degrees of power—one lesser, untruthful power consisting of the pairs of opposites (everything of this world), and a second, greater or 'almighty' power of truth which can overcome the lesser bad power and multiply its good.

So many spiritual seekers write saying they have an 'appearance' of migraine, or cancer, or a broken bone, or loneliness, or depression, or lack, or insecurity, or homelessness, or family discord or fear, for which they ask healing. If only these people knew the truth, they would never ask for such an objective and localized healing but for *illumined senses*. It is illumined sense that enables one to see the untouched and eternal truth of the body.

None of truth can be made evident in or from or for or through an appearance believed to be an actual entity or condition because everything of appearance is one hundred percent illusory, just as the joined-together railway tracks are one hundred percent illusory.

Spiritual students have latched onto the word 'appearance' and now make *it* an entity and power they want to be rid of. The power of a mental or physical or material problem has now been dropped for the power of 'appearance', which has become the fashionable problem to be healed, harmonized, prospered, or pacified. But do you see that if we have an 'appearance' to be healed, we still have two powers—the 'lesser' power of an appearance versus the 'greater' power of truth, truth being able to overcome 'appearance'?

Truth, which is *all*, contains nothing but itself—no 'appearance', no 'other' under any circumstances or conditions whatsoever, not even temporarily as 'you' or a particular moment of your experience. All but God itself is illusory appearance, nothing more, nothing different (if we believe it to be an actual entity, an actual 'something' that has its own power, quality and condition). Appearance, because it *is* nothing but appearance, needs no more 'done' about it than images on the movie screen need something done about them.

ONE PRESENCE

There is just one presence, one power, one quality, one amount, one condition, one being, one body, one form.

Everything that appears isn't in and of its own self *that one*, so forget appearance. Forget it, and instead do this:

Instantly realize that any and every appearance—the whole of it, including all its detail—'just is' and is therefore of no consequence. It has no power because only God is power. It has no quality because only God is quality. It has no body or form or amount or function because only God is body, form, amount and function. It has no activity or condition because only God is activity and condition. It has no 'good' quality or 'bad' quality because only God is. It has no 'constructive' quality or 'destructive' quality because only God is. It has no 'abundant' quality or 'lacking' quality because only God is. It has no 'healthy' quality or 'unhealthy' quality because only God is. It has no 'intelligent' or 'unintelligent' quality because only God is. It has no 'presence' or 'absence' because only God is. It isn't a 'he, she or it' because only God is. It isn't 'human, animal, vegetable, mineral, cell, atom, sub-atomic particle or quantum field' because only God is.

Then in a state of detached and untroubled consciousness—no belief in, no love, hate or fear of the appearance—rest in the deep stillness and silence of God-is and *there* witness, *feel*, the presence of God.

You may experience God as a feeling of peace welling up within or of love or joy or harmony or freedom or light or warmth or heat permeating your body or an area of the body. You may experience God as a truth statement suddenly filling your senses or as an instruction either audible or inaudible.

There are boundless ways in and as which God can be experienced, so don't limit your expectation. Stay silent, open and receptive, *expecting* a God experience of one sort or another.

As soon as you have it, the 'healing'—the revealing of

truth—is complete. The fog of discordant or diseased appearance is 'cleared' and revealed to be truthful appearance. In our example of a person calling with a headache, we instantly recognize the *whole* experience being presented to us as nothing more than falsely-sensed God. Both the person *and* the headache are experiencing each other because of false God-sense or mis-identity that, in and of its own self, requires no understanding and no dealing with. The person presenting himself is neither good nor bad; nor does he have anything good or bad happening 'to' him; and the headache the person arrived with is neither good nor bad. The experience presenting itself is just an 'is' of material (false) sense. Neither the person nor the headache has any quality or condition of its own because only God is and has quality and condition. The whole appearance 'just is,' which is nothing but illusory sense.

In this 'just is' realization you are untroubled and detached, spacious and peaceful and full of God, instantly 'inviting' the truthful experience of man to become evident. Your presence of truth *is* the truth-revealing influence. In and as the openness, silence and receptivity of your being, truth reveals itself where untruth appeared to exist in this man's experience. His experience becomes healthy, harmonious and free of discord, not only, in this case, of the headache, but of *all* false experience.

OUR WORK THIS WEEK

Realize more deeply the non-reality of all appearance, all of experience *in and of its own self.*

Detach ever more from everything that appears to be, everything of experience, both 'good' and 'bad.'

Become less and less troubled by any and every experience of either good or bad in the realization that, despite appearance, only God is, and God is the actuality of you and your world this minute, in every most practical way.

In the realization of God-is, rest more, be silent more, be receptive to the 'inner presence' of truth forever giving you all of itself and forever revealing itself as your every sense, your being, mind, body and world and everything in it and of it—truth *being* the fullness of itself as the fullness of you.

I am with you twenty-four hours a day, holding the light of truth for you, the light that you and your world are.

Let the light of truth see for you.

Rest back in God itself, rely on God itself, trust God itself happening as you, "closer than breathing and nearer than hands and feet."

CONSCIOUSNESS IS THE MIRACLE

❖

If you have devoted the suggested one week to contemplating and really *working with* each chapter's truth message, you have beautifully enriched and deepened awareness and are now ready for an incredible revelation.

Let's journey on it today. As you do, remember that the key to spiritual awakening is *depth* and *vitality* of truth awareness taking good, strong root in well-fertilized 'ground'—being—growing forth, blossoming, then bearing fruit as individual consciousness.

It is the spiritually lifted and enriched being that bears fruit richly, experiencing the good of life unbounded and unconditional, with "twelve baskets full left over." Therefore, read slowly, purposefully, richly. Savor each sentence, each nuance, each truth. Take in the treasure each page offers you. Relish the message as "the pearl of great price," for indeed it is.

CONSCIOUSNESS DESCRIBED AS "THE EARTH"

"The earth" in our statement "The earth is the Lord's and the fullness thereof" means *consciousness*—the earthly, three-dimensional, five-sensory awareness of God, the God-experience, that which we call 'human' and 'worldly'—mental, physical, material.

Everything, infinitely, is consciousness. The reference to earth is a reference to consciousness. So it can be understood that, "consciousness is the Lord's and the fullness thereof."

Whenever you have a question about God or anything about your sense of you or your world, come back to the foundation of truth: God is consciousness, and because God is infinite and omnipresent, there is "none else" but consciousness.

We can go further and understand the word "Lord" as meaning mind. We now have: "The earth [consciousness] is the Lord's [mind's] and the fullness thereof." God is mind is formation (earth); therefore, all of experience is consciousness experiencing itself, and the subject and object of experience are the *fullness* of consciousness. The whole of God—consciousness which is infinity and omnipresence—is present at every point of itself simultaneously.

So let us understand this: *everything* in and of individual consciousness, your consciousness and mine, everything, everything, *everything*—whether a mountain or a speck of dust, an ocean or a dew drop, a human being or a nanobe, an entire body or a single cell or atom, every being in the universe or one, all the money in the world or a penny, a billion miles or an inch, all the space in the cosmos or all the space within an atom, all the time in eternity or this one millisecond—everything we can name and experience, without exception, is consciousness witnessed *as and being itself.*

At the 'human' degree of awareness, consciousness is experienced conceptually. Our experience is formed of three-dimensional and five-sensory mind. Mind *is* formation, and because mind at our degree of it is three-dimensional and of five senses, our formed experience is three-dimensional and of five senses. The three-dimensional and five-sense awareness provides our experience with subjectivity, objectivity, locality and finiteness—a multitudinally populated world and universe existing in time and space, consisting of cause and effect.

The most important thing to realize about experience—the world and universe and everything in and of and about it, including everything about you and every 'him, her and it' that is today and ever can be in your experience—is that *it of its own self is unconditioned and innocent.*

Because God *is* mind *is* formation (earth and universe and every being and thing everywhere in it and of it, without exception), *all is God* and *of* God. Nothing of God, mind or formation (earth) is anything but the *fullness* of God. Oh, if you can understand this you will walk right into your truth and freedom this day!

All is *pure consciousness being the fullness and omnipresence of itself at every point of infinity at the same time.* The formed experience of God—the human, earthly experience—cannot, nor does it, 'change' or 'lessen' or 'dilute' or 'finitize' or 'localize' God. We are simply having a corporeal or earthly *sense* of that which is always one hundred percent God. But that sense does not, nor can, 'change' God and what is God's. The only being, mind and formation is God, therefore spiritual and "very good"—pure and beautiful, bountiful and purposeful, innocent and unbounded.

When we observe any and every him, her, it, activity, amount, place and condition, what we are observing is God and the fullness of God because there is nothing but God, therefore nothing but God to observe or experience: "He that sees me sees him that sent [is] me....[1] For in him we live, and move, and have our being..."[2] and God lives and moves and has his being in and as me (because God is the only). "The earth is the Lord's and the fullness

---

[1] John 12:45   [2] Acts 17:28

thereof."

Only when we add *belief* to experience do we suffer because belief about experience instantaneously separates us *in sense* from God. As soon as we separate our senses from God, we are out in the pairs of opposites, lost and lonely, exposed to a multitude of believed good and bad powers, places and conditions. This is what the Master explained to us in the parable of the prodigal son. We believe that something other than God exists or that something other than God is being our experience.

Humanity has never understood that it itself— and its world and universe itself—is the very presence of God, oneness (because there is "none other"), simply experienced as conceptual mind formation. It has always believed that appearance is something different from, or less than, or separate from God itself. It has never taken *literally* the truth given it by every spiritual light of the ages: God is all, in all, as all, and through all—the very presence and formation of all.

There is none but God, infinity and omnipresence! Mind is God-mind because nothing other than God is; and because all formation is of mind, all formation is, and is as full of God as mind is.

If we believe that experience—anything and everything of experience—is something of *its own self,* a separate, self-contained and self-operating entity, with its own nature, quality and power, that belief means we have God 'and' matter, God 'and' humanity, God 'and' body, organ and function, God 'and' money, God 'and' relationship and so on in sense. And because sense *is* experience, what we believe about sense *is* our sensed experience.

What appears to be human *isn't;* it is God because only God is. What appears to be finite *isn't;* it is infinity because only God, infinity is. What appears to be local and separate *isn't;* it is the oneness of omnipresence because only God is and God is one and omnipresent. What appears to be objectified, 'an object' *isn't;* it is simply objectified *sense* of omnipresence, the whole of God, therefore the whole of unconditioned good, life, harmony, abundance, peace and fulfillment of being and experience.

The truth of all, without exception, and without even the possibility of exception, is God, pure consciousness. The whole of God *is being* the whole*ness* of all being, mind, body, world and universe, and everything everywhere in and of it. The whole *is* fully existent and formed at every point of itself at the same time.

All is one infinite whole *being wholly itself*—pure, omnipresent consciousness. You are that, I am that, all is that. You and your entire world are the one whole of being. "I am that I am." Wherever you look, there I am; whatever you sense, it is I; whatever you see, hear, taste, touch, smell or think it is I and the fullness of I.

CONSCIOUSNESS IS THE MIRACLE

We do not have our 'own' consciousness. There is no consciousness but God consciousness, and God cannot be divided into many or into parts. God is eternally one and whole, omnipresent, indivisible and inseparable from any of itself. If it were possible for God to divide or separate itself, or make itself in any way different or less, God never would have been one, but many. That is untrue and impossible. One is one, period, and indeed, one is what God is. I am one, and besides me there is none other.

This awareness of *no consciousness being 'mine,' all consciousness being God, therefore God's* is a giant leap in awakening. "The earth [consciousness] is the Lord's [God itself] and the fullness thereof." Nothing but the fullness exists. When we catch even a *grain* of what this truly means, we begin to experience a freedom of being never imagined possible.

> *Your consciousness is FULL of*
> *and overflowing with miracles.*

> *Consciousness IS the presence*
> *and miracle of God. Consciousness IS God.*

> *Your consciousness and the fullness thereof*
> *IS the one eternal miracle of God, already fully*
> *manifested and demonstrated, visible*
> *and tangible. There is none other.*

You have been searching for a miracle that you have believed will heal your life, yet the very consciousness you have been searching with *is itself the omnipresence of inexhaustible miracles*—the one great and unconditional miracle of God itself being everything you are, everything you have, and everything you experience—inclusive of the subject and object, activity and amount of your experience.

Every speck of consciousness is alive as, and full of God—infinite and omnipresent good, life, beauty, bounty, love, joy and freedom. Your entire consciousness—every breath, moment and particle of it—is a miracle of inestimable proportions. And because consciousness *is* experience, your entire *experience* is a miracle of inestimable proportions, alive as, and full of God.

Ah, but you say it isn't! And I say to you, how *aware* are you of the miracle of God as all? Experiencing *truth* is all about being *aware* of God as all. Only that which you are *aware of* can and does exist in your experience; that which you are *unaware of,* even it stands right next to you in all its glory, is not and cannot be in your experience.

Every breath, every place, every aspect, every moment of your awareness—everywhere infinitely, as far as your imagination can go, whatever you are doing and whomever or whatever you're doing it with, wherever you go and whatever you see, hear, taste, touch or smell—is the presence of the *whole* of God. God is unconditionally available to the God-aware as all the formation and ingredients of experience, already and fully manifested, demonstrated, tangible and visible as all.

God is you, me and all, ever 'seeking' to be fully revealed as and through your presence—ever seeking to pierce material sense to reveal truthful sense just as the new light of dawn pierces the shadows of earth.

CONSCIOUS AWARENESS IS THE KEY

Consciousness—omnipresence—requires *awareness* of *it itself as all* to be visibly and tangibly real in experience, to be real as the palpable "image and likeness" of God as experience.

Let us understand this deeper than ever before, otherwise all the continued truth-knowing on earth will not, and cannot, become evident in individual or collective experience.

If you have thoroughly understood the message so far, you know that God—consciousness—is all there is, that oneness is the only existence inclusive of the only *formation* of existence. You know that God *is* mind *is* formation, the one and oneness of all, and that, therefore, you are that, I am that, all is that *and the fullness thereof.* You know that nothing but the omnipresent *whole simultaneously exists* at every point of itself.

From hereon, to understand the infinite forms, aspects,

activities and ingredients of conceptual (earthly) experience—that which has been named 'mental, physical, material, earthly, universal, subjective and objective'—realize
that *all describable form*, all of *experience*, is simply mind-ex-
perience at 'this' degree of awareness called human. It is
one of the "many mansions [degrees of awareness] in my
Father's house [the infinity of consciousness]."

Each degree of awareness is a whole universe unto itself. Everything in and of that degree is itself infinity, omnipresence and eternity—the whole of God omnipresent,
simply being experienced as that particular degree of
awareness.

God is not less or more present in any particular degree of awareness. The *whole* is invariably present as all,
and cannot be less so, or differently so. The *whole* is forever *one and complete as* every degree and moment, every
subject and object of awareness—inseparably, indivisibly
and unconditionally *one*, just as wetness is to water, and
water is to wetness.

The *less* you are consciously aware of this great truth,
the *less is your experience of it* as the good of your mind, body
and world; the *more* you are consciously aware of truth,
the *more is your experience of it* as the good of your mind,
body and world—your tangibly experienced health,
wealth, love, happiness, peace, joy, purpose and fulfillment of being. It is all about *awareness*.

There is no such thing as unexpressed, unmanifested,
undemonstrated, invisible or intangible awareness. Awareness *is forever* expressed, manifest, demonstrated, visible
and tangible because it is nothing less than a degree of
that which is the one, eternally expressed, manifested,
demonstrated, visible and tangible existence: God or consciousness.

In other words, awareness is within consciousness, not

separate or apart, not a different aspect of being. We are simply having a degree of awareness of that which is forever *the one and omnipresent* manifested, visible and tangible whole. Therefore, any and every degree of awareness is itself, and contains, the *whole* (because consciousness, without exception, is whole at every point of itself at the same time).

Oneness is oneness! Omnipresence is omnipresence! There is *none else.* There is no*where else.* There is no other choice. God *is*, and there is no degree of awareness *or unawareness* that isn't actually full of God. There is no mind, body, place, activity, amount or condition 'other' than God. Where would that 'other' exist in literal oneness and omnipresence? It would not, cannot, and does not—not even in belief. However, awareness or unawareness is the difference between an experience visibly and tangibly filled with God, good, versus an experience lacking the visibility and tangibility of God.

So realize that because all is consciousness being the whole of itself—oneness and omnipresence being its and the only mind, body, place, activity, amount and condition—there is no 'other' state or place or type of experience consciousness 'changes into' or 'fills' or 'makes' manifest, 'makes' tangible, 'makes' visible or 'demonstrates.' All is one, forever whole and manifest, already and eternally demonstrated, vibrantly visible and tangible. Nothing 'still has to happen.' All already *is* and 'has happened.'

There is not God *and.* There is not a spiritual being and world *and* a material being and world which spirit somehow fills or heals or harmonizes or prospers or pacifies. Spirit does not change bad, lacking or unhealthy matter into good, abundant and healthy matter. *There is no matter; there is only spirit—God, spirit and truth.*

Remember until it radiates from your every cell and breath—we are simply having a material *sense* of that which is one hundred percent spirit. Sense does not, nor ever can, 'change' spirit into matter. All is God, spirit and truth, and our sense *without belief about it* is one hundred percent innocent and impotent. Therefore, without belief about it, the corporeally-sensed experience of God, the 'this world' experience, is equally one hundred percent innocent and impotent.

All is one, and that one is consciousness—the whole of itself being your very consciousness, your very being—fully manifested, tangible, visible and *happening as* you and your reality, for where 'else' could omnipresent oneness be other than right here?

Indeed! Omnipresent oneness is not only 'right here' but is itself—the *whole* of God—happening as you and every moment and form of your entire experience. "I [consciousness] am that [you and your entire mind, body and world] I am."

DEGREE OF AWARENESS

You now understand that whatever *degree* of awareness you *consciously have*—or we can say, you are consciously *being*—is itself your manifest, tangible, visible experience.

Every moment of you and your experience, no matter how good or bad, illumined or dark your awareness, is the fullness of God, fully manifested and visibly present. *However,* your 'amount' or degree of *awareness* inescapably determines *how much* of the manifested and visible truth you tangibly witness. The whole of truth is exactly where you are this minute, but *seeing—awareness* of *it as all*—is the key.

How *full* of God, good, is your experience? The answer will depend on your degree of awareness of truth 'happening' and omnipresent as you and your world—as the one, omnipresent substance and formation of all experience.

Realize that—despite the degree of lack or limitation, pain or suffering you or your world may be experiencing this moment—right here where you are this minute is the fullness of unconditional God, good, the miracle of God as individual being and experience (of you and everything in your world), the perfectly visible and real manifestation of God as all "as far as your eye can see."

"AS FAR AS THE EYE CAN SEE"

The scriptural reference "as far as the eye can see" means, by the degree of truth you are *consciously aware of*, you are consciously *being*, as far 'into and throughout' experience your degree of truth-awareness takes you. *Conscious awareness* is the entire key.

Imagine that I blindfolded you and took you to my favorite place on earth. You have never been to this place— you have no conscious awareness of it—so when we arrive, we each have a completely *different awareness*, therefore *experience*, of the same place. A familiar joy runs through my being. It is my favorite place so I have spent much time here. I am familiar with, and appreciate its beauty, peace, scenery, its geography, its rich foliage and abundant flowers, colors, fragrances, character, activity, sound, its pathways, nooks and crannies, its feel.

You have no awareness of it. You have never been here before, and you are blindfolded so your experience is 'dark.'

Now let's say I cut a small hole in the blindfold. Suddenly you are able to see a little of this place, have a little more *conscious awareness* of it. You are now able to *experience* a greater degree of it. Being consciously aware is your tangible experience, so you can begin to describe that which you now have *conscious awareness of*, whereas a moment ago you had little or no conscious awareness (of that which you couldn't see). Because you were *unaware*, you had little or no experience.

Now let's say I cut a hole two or three times larger. You now have two or three times the degree of conscious awareness of this place; therefore, your tangible experience is now two or three times greater. Finally the blindfold is removed and you have full conscious awareness, therefore unhindered *experience*, of the place "whereon we stand."

The only difference between *full* experience and *no* or *little* experience is the degree of individual *conscious awareness* we each have. Equally we can understand that if either you or I were asleep in this place, we would be unconscious of it, therefore unable to have a conscious experience of it.

In all these examples the place remains the same—the fullness of itself, the fully manifested, demonstrated, tangible and visible presence and formation of the place. It is simply, and only, the *degree of conscious awareness* we each individually have—we each are *being*—that determines our individual *tangible experience* of it. Awareness *is* tangible experience.

Is this clearer now?

Truth awareness works in exactly this way. God, truth, is *fully present, formed and visible* here, now and forever right where you are, as and throughout your experience—*being* itself *as* the entirety of you, your world and universe—just as my favorite place is fully present, formed and visible.

"The place whereon you stand is holy (whole, omnipresent) ground." You are the *fullness* of God, the whole of infinity and omnipresence being itself as you and your world.

Your versus my individual experience is entirely dependent on the degree of *conscious awareness of truth* we individually have, or *are being* moment-by- moment, hour-by-hour, day-by-day.

The truth that God is fully present, manifested and visible doesn't help our experience of it in the slightest until we each, individually, become *consciously aware* of it.

By the degree we become consciously aware of God as all, we experience the good of God by that degree—no less, no more, no different.

SCIENCE OF TRUTH

Truth, being principle, is an *exact science* just as the principle of mathematics or aerodynamics or gravity is. We 'get' what we 'give to' any principle; we 'receive' the degree we are being aware of; we experience the degree of truth we are *consciously being.*

The more we know—are consciously aware of—the truth of mathematics or aerodynamics or gravity, the more these principles 'give' us. The more we are consciously aware of and act in accordance with them, the more of their fullness is revealed—manifest, visible and tangible to us—therefore the more of their qualities and freedom of expression and form we have available as our experience.

CONSCIOUS AWARENESS OF THE MIRACLE REVEALS THE MIRACLE

Because God is consciousness, because the whole of God is present at every point of itself simultaneously, and because the consciousness every individual is and has is

God consciousness—indivisible, therefore whole, forever manifest, visible and tangible—individual consciousness is full of the miracle of God. Individual consciousness *is* the miracle of God, and becomes perfectly visible and real for you and everyone to see wherever you let *it itself* live as you and every form of experience.

Every grain of your consciousness *is* the miracle of God, your utter fulfillment of being. Every subject and object of your awareness—despite its appearance—is a miracle of unbridled beauty, bounty, life, love, peace, purpose and fulfillment.

But this truth—this fact—does you no good unless you are *consciously aware* of the miracle everywhere present. We can state it like this: the fact that truth is true doesn't 'show' in experience unless it is *being consciously and constantly realized.*

Awareness *is* the visibility and tangibility—the reality—of truth in experience. This is the great key to the God-experienced life, to true spiritual awakening, to harmonious and purposeful being.

OUR WORK THIS WEEK

Become more and more *consciously aware* of God being all. Every moment, point and place of your consciousness is the miracle of God itself—the omnipresence of God as omni-being, omni-mind and omni-form (earth, universe), unconditionally you and yours for the good of all.

You have life as individual God-being. "Ye are gods, and all of you are children of the most high."[1] Your purpose is God-purpose—to forever reveal the glory of God as all, heaven as earth. "Whether therefore ye eat, or drink, or whatsoever ye do, do all to the glory of God."[2] Realize ever more each day that the multitudinous forms, activi-

[1] Psalm 82:6   [2] 1 Corinthians 10:31

ties and amounts of experience are *in and of their own selves* nothing; yet, despite appearance, are *actually* the very presence of God. Forever realize that we are having a corporeal *sense* of the incorporeal. Realize that sensed experience at face value, and if believed, is false and 'without' God. It is *God awareness* that makes God *evident* in experience. "Judge not by the appearance, but judge righteous judgment."[1] When all is understood to be the presence and formation of God—"righteous judgment"— the whole of God is 'released' to be freely visible, tangible and real in experience.

Remember, nothing of appearance—of either good or bad—has a nature, quality, power or ability of its own self because only God is; therefore, only God has nature, quality, power and ability. Ignore all appearance—both the seeming problem and its seeming solution—and *seek God, spirit, the "kingdom of heaven"* instead.

Seek the one reality, the one truth that exists here and now as everything everywhere of your consciousness. The unbounded freedom and joy of truthful being, body and world are perfectly and naturally 'available' to every individual who truthfully identifies God as being all. It is your *conscious awareness* of this great truth—the one truth—that opens the doorway of truthful experience, revealing "a land of milk and honey." It is *conscious awareness of God as all* that opens and reveals "the earth full of the goodness of God."

Develop the discipline this week and forevermore of turning your attention to God, to be aware of God itself as all—your consciousness itself as all that God is and has. Indeed, your consciousness—the consciousness of *every* being, the *one* consciousness—*is itself* the presence and formation of God as experience. Consciousness *is itself* the presence and unconditional miracle of God as all. Noth-

[1] John 7:24

ing has to be 'done' about it, or 'brought forth' into experience. God is already 'done' and 'brought forth'! God is all (God *is* mind *is* formation), and because there is no unmanifested or undemonstrated, invisible or intangible God, all of experience is already all that God is. *Awareness* of this truth is the secret of witnessing it.

Turn within twenty, thirty, fifty, one hundred times every twenty-four hours, until you are doing so without thinking, to bring attention to consciousness itself being all—God itself as all.

Also have more and longer periods of time each day in which you devote your whole self to *silence*. *Feel* God—silence—happening within. Be still, and peaceful, and receptive many times throughout the day, letting God get on with being God as you in and as and 'through' your silence. God is silence, so yield to silence time and time again each day. Then the unconditional gifts and treasures of God open up everywhere you are, visible to all, and for all.

"The earth is the Lord's and the fullness thereof."

THE FIELDS ARE ALREADY
WHITE FOR HARVEST

We now delve more deeply still into our second truth statement, "The earth is the Lord's and the fullness thereof," by opening our being to one of the greatest spiritual lessons ever given mankind—'mankind' being the three-dimensional sense of God, the 'human, material, physical, conceptual, earthly' sense of being.

We find ourselves 2000 years ago—which is taking place in you right now, for there is only *now*—in the city of Samaria watching the Master talking with the woman by the well:

> It was about the sixth hour. A woman of Samaria came to draw water.
> Jesus said to her, Give me a drink, for His disciples had gone away into the city to buy food.
> Then the woman of Samaria said to him, How is it that you, being a Jew, ask a drink from me, a Samaritan woman? For Jews have no dealings with Samaritans.
> Jesus answered and said to her, If you knew the gift of God, and who it is who says to you, Give me a drink, you would have asked him, and he would have given you living water.

The woman said to him, Sir, you have nothing to draw with, and the well is deep. Where then do you get that living water?

You see, Jesus is not speaking of the material type of water, the material *sense* of the one spiritual substance, nor was he ever speaking of 'matter.' He was speaking of the true water, the one substance—spirit and truth. So we hear him answering her:

Whoever drinks of this water [material-type water] will thirst again, but whoever drinks of the water that I shall give him will never thirst. The water that I shall give him will become in him a fountain of water springing up into everlasting life. The woman said to him, Sir, give me this water, that I may not thirst, nor come here to draw.[1]

By now Jesus had been teaching all morning and his disciples had returned with food and urged him to eat. He lovingly turned to his friends. "I have food to eat of which you do not know,"[2] he told them.

THE ONE SUBSTANCE AND FORM

After all the time the disciples had spent with him, they still had not understood the difference between the material *sense* of spirit and the belief *about* that sense—in this instance, material food versus spirit itself. They hadn't yet awakened to the truth that only God is, only oneness is, and that all form is actually, despite appearance, the very presence of God, spirit—omnipresent infinity.

Yes, *I have food to eat of which you do not know.* My food is spirit *felt* welling up within, filling and fulfilling my ex-

[1] John 4:7-15   [2] John 4:32

perience of being. My being is *tangibly fulfilled* as I sit still and silent, receptive to and being filled with spiritual experience—the *feeling* of God happening within me, as me. That feeling *is* the experience of fulfillment; the feeling *is itself* the fulfillment of being.

Feeling God happening within, or as and throughout my being, *is itself* the one and only true food. It is *literal* food and *literally* feeds me with any 'type' of food at any degree of awareness I am currently living. It feeds me without the appearance of an objectified food agency (material food) if my realization of the one true food—spirit and truth—is high and complete enough.

Or it feeds—and usually does for most people at the 'human' degree of awareness—as objective, material food. It is the same one food, just *experienced* at the particular degree of awareness the individual is living.

As God is felt happening, material food appears easily and naturally—so much so that the unenlightened often believe that nothing unusual has happened, just a good and hearty sufficiency of food witnessed for all. Take note that there is no mention of a 'miracle' taking place in either of the accounts of Jesus feeding the multitudes; the arrival of food seemed to everyone present to be perfectly natural.

It can equally appear, and sometimes does, in what the unenlightened say is a miracle. Out of the clear blue sky food becomes available where there seemed to be no 'natural' or available means for it. But appear it will and infallibly does, *when we know and rest in the truth that all form, including tangible food, is spirit and nothing different.*

When we know this—really know it—and when we rely on the experience, *the feeling of spirit and truth happening within,* then our good is experienced as whatever form represents our current fulfillment. The *happening,* the *experi-*

ence of spirit felt within is the tangible and literal food of life, no matter at what degree we are aware of it. As long as we know and rely on the truth that God is all, it doesn't matter what degree of awareness we live. All good, all fulfillment is experienced at whatever level of awareness we exist.

To illustrate this truth further for his friends, the Master went on to explain, "Do you not say, 'There are still four months and then comes the harvest'? Behold, I say to you, lift up your eyes and look at the fields, for they are already white for harvest!"[1]

Jesus is telling us not to assume there is a delay in spiritual fulfillment. Fulfillment is never delayed; fulfillment *is*. Spirit *is already and forever* the fulfillment of being in every way—fulfilled oneness, oneness being nothing but the perpetual wholeness and completeness of itself. It is utterly impossible for oneness to be partial, less than, different from, or in any way separated from any aspect or part of itself. One and oneness is always whole and fulfilled *as one and oneness*. In this way, spirit *is* here and now, already and forever fulfilled as itself no matter how the scene appears to be at any moment of sense.

Don't look 'out there' and believe what you observe as having any reality or power or season or evolutionary process to it whatsoever. What 'out there' truly is—what *all* truly is—is spirit and truth, oneness, which is already and forever one, whole, complete, manifested, demonstrated, perfect and fulfilled. Nothing 'has to happen'; all already is.

This is why the Master asks, "Do you not say, 'There are still four months and then comes the harvest?" Do you not say, because you're looking 'out there,' judging and believing what *appears to be*, that there is a delay, a season or process or method to wait for *before* you can experience fulfillment?

[1] John 4:35

"Behold, I say to you, lift up your eyes and look at the fields, for they are already white for harvest!" I say to you, spirit and truth are the only reality no matter what sense, if believed, seems to suggest. Therefore, look to spirit and truth—"look up"—for *then* you will discover that the fields, the entirety of awareness, the entirety of the material senses, are "already white for harvest," already fulfilled in every formed way, fully manifested, visible and tangible, and available to experience as fulfilled form this hour *as long as you are consciously aware of this truth.*

STOP HERE FOR A FEW DAYS: DEEPLY CONTEMPLATE THESE THREE EXTRAORDINARY TRUTH STATEMENTS

Take the next few days to contemplate these three master-truths of the Master:

1. Whoever drinks of this water will thirst again, but whoever drinks of the water that I shall give him will never thirst. The water that I shall give him will become in him a fountain of water springing up into everlasting life.

2. I have food to eat of which you do not know.

3. Do you not say, 'There are still four months and then comes the harvest'? Behold, I say to you, lift up your eyes and look at the fields, for they are already white for harvest!

Bear in mind always, Jesus told us, *God is spirit, and those who worship him must worship in spirit and truth.* He told this same truth to the woman of Samaria in explaining the nature of the true water, the true all.

Therefore—*always*—the 'food' of which he speaks, the 'flesh,' the 'bread,' the 'wine,' the 'life,' the 'currency' is spirit and truth. *That* is the real presence, the real substance, the real body, the real form, the real food, the real amount, the real peace and harmony, justice, safety and security, the only only, the *one*, even though it *appears through the five senses to be* material or physical form, finite in nature, limited in amount, variable in quality.

Contemplate this now—gently, deeply, richly. Take these incredible truths more deeply into your being than ever before! Remember, *depth* is the key to spiritual awakening, living, and 'demonstration.'

Integrate your contemplation with silent listening or attentiveness so that truth itself is able to become clear and real to you, able to become a greater living reality within you.

Then watch what wonderful experiences begin to happen during these next few days. If you really devote yourself to this contemplation, and to silence in which you *feel* spirit happening, watch the wonders and even miracles that begin to take place. Watch what reveals itself in and as and to your tangible experience. It is a "wonder to behold."

Always remember that heaven is right here *as* your very consciousness. There is no searching, no delay. There is just the need to *experience* and in that way *release as visible and tangible* that which already is.

The whole of infinity and omnipresence *is* your consciousness, perpetually *being* its whole, fulfilled presence and form—all one—as you, inclusive of your experience. As you know this truth, as you rest and relax in it and as it, and as you enable it to be your manifested reality through your regular silence of being, the fruits of heaven are ever more lavish and abundant in experience. You have awakened to reality.

Think. The whole of omnipresent infinity is already fully manifest and demonstrated as the you you are. Infinity is the presence of you, the body of you, the capacity of you, the nature and power of you. Infinity of all good form and condition is what you inherently are and have. But it is the *realization* of this great truth, and the *living of it*—the true, living reliance on *truth alone*—that 'releases' infinity, making it visible and tangible and the one reality to sense.

Ponder, ponder, and ponder ever more these extraordinary truths. Ponder them more deeply, day and night. Every *minute* of further pondering, contemplating, chewing on, and then sitting in silence to allow them to "spring forth as living waters"—to be the very tangibility of fulfillment—deepens and enriches conscious awareness of the reality of truth, therefore the realized embodiment of truthful, joyous, harmonious and free life experience; every *minute* of pondering truth and letting truth—in your silence and receptivity—abide in you achieves this in your experience.

"I am the vine, you are the branches. He who remains [abides] with me, and I with him, will bear abundant fruit; for without me [truth] you can do nothing."[1]

PART TWO

How was Jesus able to realize any and every appearing illness, lack, limitation or disharmony as being false, then promptly prove the nothingness of that appearance and the one reality of health, harmony and abundance? How did he demonstrate, beyond any doubt, that only fulfillment is?

[1] John 15:5

Let us understand this now. You have devoted a few days to pondering the truth revealed in Part One. I know that wonderful, greater clarity about these truths has and continues to spring forth for you. Now let's go more deeply:

> Whoever drinks of this water [material type water, the image and likeness of the true water] will thirst again, but whoever drinks of the water that I shall give him [spirit itself] will never thirst. The water that I shall give him will become in him a fountain of water springing up into everlasting life.

The Master is revealing the truth and freedom of being. As long as we believe and rely on the *material* degree of experience, it will forever run dry on us. All its forms become exhausted, dry and empty. We continually need to renew them, earn more of them, protect them, exert mental, physical and material effort for them and maintain them. They will never satisfy us, continually varying and proving themselves unreliable, eventually failing. They cannot and do not ever fulfill us as we have hoped they would.

Why? The mental, physical, material is not *in and of its own self* real, not an actual, separate entity or form or presence. If it is believed to be an actual and separate entity, an actual reality, its *truth* cannot be experienced. Belief itself has 'frozen' or 'imprisoned' experienced form, making it impossible for its truth—the omnipresent infinity and fulfillment of form—to be evident.

All but the experience of God itself *as all* is simply believed form, and believed form is as empty of the evidence of God as dark is empty of light.

God is eternally omnipresent as all form and openly

available as the "image and likeness" of itself for all to experience. But if belief is on the scene, that belief imprisons the believer's experience to be the very 'type' and 'quality' and 'nature' of form he's believing.

> Yet… "whoever drinks of the water that I shall give him [God itself, spirit and truth itself, the one true fulfillment] will never thirst. The water that I shall give him will become in him a fountain of water springing up into everlasting life."

You now see why illumined awareness is able to say, quite literally, *I have food to eat of which you do not know.* The only true food is God itself—spirit and truth itself. When we live on and by spirit and truth, we discover—by the degree we're living it—that it literally feeds us with everything needed for complete fulfillment and purpose of being. Every resource is already here "before you call" and exactly when and how we need it, including every meal exactly when we and however many friends we are with this hour, need *it.*

More and more—as spiritual awareness increases, and material conviction decreases—fulfillment satisfies the material sense of experience without the 'agency' of the seemingly required material form.

For instance, the more you live on and by the true, one food of spirit and truth, the more you discover that the material agency (image) of food—the material "meat, wine, and water"—is not needed.

Spirit and truth experienced 'happening' literally "feeds" the experience of body without material food. The true body is incorporeal—spirit alone—and is eternally fed and fulfilled. Why then, would it require material food? It doesn't, and the more we lift into a living *awareness* of our true being and body—that being spirit and spiritual—the less of 'material' food, health, money, love and harmony we need as our fulfillment. Although it often appears in 'material' ways, material form is never sought for its own sake. Only spirit is; therefore only spirit is sought *and experienced*—whether the *unenlightened* call that experience 'spiritual' or 'material.'

Mostly, during our rising into spiritual awareness, the agency is still needed. There is much evidence that Jesus included at least a little 'material' food in his diet although much of the time, probably mostly, he was satisfied by the "food that ye know not of." But whether food is experienced inclusive or exclusive of form, *all food is spirit and spiritual* because all is God.

A discussion about form versus no form or 'pure spirit' is irrelevant. All is God, and we are told by the Master, "Make the inner the outer, and make the outer the inner." In other words, stop believing and comparing what appears to be 'outer' form versus 'inner' spirit because if you do, you will make for yourself a "divided house" which will very often prove itself empty of 'both' spiritual *and* material food. Only God is. Realize the *omnipresence* and *irrefutability* of this truth whether any particular presence or experience is at first judged to be 'spiritual' or 'material.' Nothing of *comparison*, of 'this-versus-that' or of 'either-or' has any truth to it. Nothing of *belief* has any truth to it, period. *All is spirit*, *all is one*, and there is none other than spirit and oneness.

And so, in and as the consciousness of oneness, the experience of nourishment is always fulfilled, and always 'happens' exactly when needed and as perfect form.

DO YOU NOT SAY, "THERE ARE STILL FOUR MONTHS?"

"Do you not say, There are still four months and then comes the harvest? Behold, I say to you, lift up your eyes and look at the fields, for they are already white for harvest!"[1]

The Master is explaining that if we continue to look out at the material scene and believe it, we enslave ourselves, including the forms of our experience, in the prison of that belief—in materiality and its laws, its methods, seasons, processes, its time and space, its pairs of good and bad opposites, of presence and absence. *Do you not say [believe], There are still four months and then comes the harvest? . . . Whoever drinks of this water [material belief] will thirst again*—for all the truth of life.

But the moment it is recognized that only God, spirit and truth is, and that the whole of God and everything God has is omnipresent fulfillment of mind and form right where you are this minute and at every point and place of your existence simultaneously, the freedom of being has been discovered.

"Do not judge by the appearance, but judge righteous judgment." Judge—know—that God *alone* is, that spirit, truth and omnipresent infinity *alone* is.

No person, object, amount, activity, organization or condition—that which is name-able—can bind you, limit you, delay you, overwhelm you, disturb or destroy you from *the moment* you catch the great truth that God alone is. This being true, Yes! "I have food to eat of which you do not know." Yes! "Whoever drinks of the water that I shall give him will never thirst. The water that I shall give him will become in him a fountain of water springing up into everlasting life." Yes! "I say to you, lift up your eyes and look at

[1] John 4:35

the fields, for they are already white for harvest!"

HOW CAN TRUTH BE TRUE WHEN BY MATERIAL EVIDENCE IT PLAINLY IS NOT?

How can spiritually illumined being say to material sense, "Food is already prepared and ready for you to feast on," when according to physical evidence it plainly is not, and the only means of acquiring it is by mental and physical effort and material money?

Material sense, observing a lack of material food, believes that something 'still has to happen' in order for food to be present. All the truth in the universe hasn't brought food to the real world I am experiencing, it says.

You say, 'There are still four months and then comes the harvest.' There's the reason food seems to lack.

Whatever individual or collective being believes, *is so* in its experience. Belief *is experience.*

God, consciousness—despite the way it seems to be, or seems to be acting, or the way it appears to be present or absent in sensed experience—is the *only* and *one* substance and form. That substance and form is forever manifested and visible, demonstrated and tangible. There is no unmanifested or undemonstrated or invisible or intangible aspect or presence or form of God. However, if you believe form itself to be reality, instead of God alone as reality, you not only seek a false sense of form, but you seek it in the wrong place. *Nothing is present or happening but consciousness;* therefore there is no form other than the form of consciousness.

Illumined (spiritual) being knows that the only true food—the only true fulfillment in and of any form and amount—is God, spirit, truth; and knows that God, being omnipresent, is fully here now as all conceiveable form (and as an infinity of form not yet conceived).

There *literally* is nothing but God, spirit and truth being the entirety of your being, mind, body and world and every atom, thing, activity, amount, place and condition of it. There is *literally* and in the most practical way nothing but the omnipresent infinity of God, good, despite the way experience is believed to be by unenlightened being.

God is here, now, everywhere about, in full and glorious formation, boundlessly and unconditionally available to all. Never will the fulfilling form of experience happen 'tomorrow, next week, next month, one year from now,' or even one minute from now. *God is, right now.* Never is the fulfillment of God experienced or even experience-*able* in the future—not even a future sixty seconds away.

Now God is, and *now* it is that God must be realized and experienced.

GOD IS NOW

God is, now. God is *now. God is, now!*

Oh, just dwelling on God-is-now in the realization that God is everything—literally everything everywhere—fills us with such peace, harmony, joy and freedom, welling up within, bursting forth, flowing over, permeating all of experience!

You need nothing other than *God-is-now* because there isn't anything but God as all, now. Therefore, when you have God *consciously living as all of your awareness*, you have the infinity and omnipresence of God formation everywhere you are, and as the resource for everything you do.

When will you awaken to this almighty truth of truths? Why not *now?* The whole of God is happening as the entire experience of you this very minute, and forever. Simply accept it! Simply wake up to it, be aware of nothing 'else' and desire nothing else.

Do not desire physical health and vitality, youthful body, plentiful material food, abundant money, loving relationship, satisfying companionship and friend, successful career, home, family, community, or peaceful world. These are all the *water that satisfies not.* "Whoever drinks of this water will thirst again."

Desire God alone, pure consciousness or presence alone—the conscious awareness of the presence of infinity and omnipresence alone, 'happening' as everything you are and everything you experience.

The fields of pure consciousness are always plump with fruit and white for harvest despite material 'evidence' to the contrary. Material evidence is nothing but a state of dim or foggy belief veiling the whole and unconditional presence of God (fulfillment) as experience. Always remember that.

Take that statement and emblazon it in your memory so that you never forget it: *Material evidence is nothing but a state of dim or foggy belief veiling the whole and unconditional presence of God (fulfillment) as experience.*

Look into your life and realize that *all* 'evidence' of disease, lack, limitation, discord or disharmony is nothing more than a state of false belief—the belief in *presence* being something of its own self, separate from, or different from, or less than God. There can be no greater mis-belief or false experience. Truth is fully present in all its perfect and fulfilled form right where you are, but *material sense cannot detect it.* That's all. Experiencing fulfillment is just a matter of seeing rightly—spiritually. "Open his eyes that he may see."

Material perception is not real, not true. Material sense has no substance, law or principle to uphold or sustain it.

The very moment illumined—spiritual—consciousness arrives on the scene, truth is witnessed. Good and sufficiency, wholeness and harmony stand right there for everyone to see and benefit from and share with all others. "Lift up your eyes and look at the fields, for they are already white for harvest!"

Lift up . . . lift up . . . *lift up your senses!* Lift up your awareness to God-alone-is! Stop believing, reacting to, and therefore being limited by, whatever the material scene appears to consist of—whether presence or absence. *Look up* and *there* you find that *God is*, and the fullness thereof. "The earth is the Lord's and the fullness thereof."

OUR WORK THIS WEEK

Realize that God alone is.

Nothing 'else' is. Only God is, in the most literal and practical way. Deeply ponder this truth. Realize the *nowness* of God-alone-is. You need nothing—literally nothing—but the conscious awareness of God alone, consciousness alone, *presence* alone. Despite all material evidence to the contrary, the fullness of God is present right where you are, *as* you and every fulfilled form of your experience, this minute and forever. Therefore—again literally—all good and eternally whole being, body, thing, amount, activity, place, position and condition is present with you, and as your entire experience, this minute and always.

You are the fulfillment and freedom of being, the presence of God-being, being itself as the form and character of you. You are the "image and likeness" of God itself because there is "none else." *Only God is,* therefore the is-ness of you is *that,* and the fullness thereof. "I am that I am."

"The earth is the Lord's and the fullness thereof." You never need concern yourself with the physical, the material, the earthly. You never need concern yourself with the fulfillment of the material plane. As extraordinary or even unbelievable as this may sound to you who are immersed in material belief and custom, it is absolutely true, and true in every most tangible and applicable way.

Jesus, Gautama and every enlightened being has given us and proven this very principle of being on a mass scale. Yet, the world of material belief has rejected it and is still today infertile to it, unable to hear it, or even wanting to hear it. It wants God for improved or healed material conditions. It wants to 'use' God for its purpose, its good, and even its prejudice.

Yet awakening spiritual being quickly hears the Master as he lovingly instructs:

22. Take no thought for your life, what ye shall eat; neither for the body, what ye shall put on. 23. The life is more than meat, and the body is more than raiment.

24. Consider the ravens: for they neither sow nor reap; which neither have storehouse nor barn; and God feeds them: how much more are ye better than the fowls?

25. And which of you with taking thought can add to his stature one cubit?

26. If ye then be not able to do that thing which is least, why take ye thought for the rest?

27. Consider the lilies how they grow: they toil not, they spin not; and yet I say unto you, that Solomon in all his glory was not arrayed like one of these.

28. If then God so clothe the grass, which is to day in the field, and to morrow is cast into the oven;

how much more will he clothe you, O ye of little faith?

29. And seek not ye what ye shall eat, or what ye shall drink, neither be ye of doubtful mind.

30. For all these things do the nations of the world seek after: and your Father knows that ye have need of these things.

31. But rather seek ye the kingdom of God; and all these things shall be added unto you.

32. Fear not, little flock; for it is your Father's good pleasure to give you the kingdom.

33. Sell that ye have, and give alms; provide yourselves bags which wax not old, a treasure in the heavens that fails not, where no thief approaches, neither moth corrupts.

34. For where your treasure is, there will your heart be also.[1]

Ponder these truths deeply. Make them your hourly food and water and wine, the light of your being, the very substance of your presence.

Take them as your love, engage in the most passionate love affair with them. Ponder your love morning, noon and night. Honor them, serve them, lavish them with your attention and listening ear. And finally, give them freedom to *be* themselves as you, and to love you with their boundless gifts, by silencing your sense of self many times throughout each day.

In the silence of being, I am.

In the silence of experience, I am fully visible.

[1] Luke 12:22-34

UNDER THE GOVERNMENT
OF GOD

✤

Just a blink away from your immediate comprehension is the true you living in the true world of spirit and peace, joy and harmony, love and purpose. The true kingdom of you and all—the only actual kingdom, the kingdom of God, the kingdom of love, the kingdom of heaven as earth—exists fully manifest and real just a blink deeper than material sense.

Every infinitesimal detail is in place, pre-prepared for you—*I prepare a place for you. . . .*[1] *Before you call I will answer.*[2] Every whisper, every breath, every step, every purpose, every activity, every fulfillment of experience is *already prepared and complete* in every way *as* you and *for* you as spiritual being.

The kingdom of God is finished not still under construction, and God's kingdom is the *only*—the *spiritual* kingdom, there being none but spirit—inseparably omnipresent *as you, as all!*

Individual and collective *awareness* of the infinity of being is forever opening and blossoming, revealing ever greater, more magnificent and majestic truths about itself. In the light of spirit aflame within, material sense fades, and truthful, loving, purposeful and free being emerges, living in a world devoid of opposites and full of the goodness of God.

[1] John 14:2   [2] Isaiah 65:24

We hear of truthful being in our first statements—*All things were made through him, and without him nothing was made that was made,*[1] and. . . *God saw every thing that he had made, and, behold, it was very good,*[2] and. . . *[His] works were finished from the foundation of the world.*[3]

FEEL THE KINGDOM "CLOSER THAN BREATHING"

Stop here for five or ten or thirty minutes—or longer if you wish to! Be still, and *feel* the finished kingdom happening as you—the whole and complete, forever fulfilled kingdom of life happening as itself, as the life you are, and the body and world you experience.

Simply feel your *presence* happening, that's all. Your presence is the *one* presence, God—omnipresence. There is no 'magic' to it. Simply be still (still the mental and physical senses) by gently bringing your attention the presence of you, the essence, the *spirit* of you, the 'happening' of your life, and begin to *feel* it happening.

You do not have to 'make' anything happen, or somehow evoke spirit. God, spirit *already is,* and is happening as the whole finished kingdom of itself, as you, twenty-four hours a day. As an inspired metaphysical teacher once said, "There is a church service going on inside of you twenty-four hours day, *but are you there?"*

Simply bring your attention, your awareness, to your presence happening, instead of on the 'outer' sense of it you have been taught to believe is reality—the mental, physical, material, objectified sense.

As you become aware of the gentle, pure presence of God happening, you will begin to feel a peace or warmth or love or sense of release and bliss well up within and fill your senses. *This is the very presence of God, spirit and truth,*

[1] John 1:3   [2] Genesis 1:31   [3] Hebrews 4:3

the kingdom of heaven being experienced as the you that you are, here and now—"earth as it is in heaven."

Feel its presence happening.

Feel its rhythm.

Feel its gentle pulse happening as you.

Feel its peace, its love, its grace happening as you.

Feel its silence. That silence is the truth of you, the oneness and completeness of you, the purpose of you fully manifested and visible, tangible and already demonstrated for you. That silence *felt happening as you* is the greatest power on earth, your greatest gift of life and love to mankind, your greatest gift of peace, harmony and freedom to earth. Nothing of God is hidden from tangible experience as *silence* lives you.

God *is* silence, silence *is* God. And because God is *one* and inseparable—that oneness being forever and wholly manifested, demonstrated, visible and tangible—all that God is and has becomes naturally experienced when silence lives "on earth." Where the presence of the Lord [silence] is, there is liberty."

Where the presence of 'noise' is, there are the pairs of opposites, "this world" with its multitudes of good *and* bad experience, its pain and suffering, the unreliable and temperamental life 'without' God.

'Noise' is *belief*—the opposite of Godliness, oneness, *silence*. 'Noise' is belief in what *seems to be*, belief in the 'outer,' objectified, 'worldly' experience of all 'hims, hers and its' being something in and of their own selves. It is the belief that every person and everything everywhere is its own, separate entity, existing among a multitude of other separate self-entities, all living and acting out their separate existence of either good or bad in degrees of success or survival.

When we are fixated on the mental, physical and material sense of existence, believing it of *its own self* to be real, we shut our experience out of the truth, freedom, omnipresence and infinity that is all around us, existing *as us* and everything of our world. Our senses are falsely attached to that which, on the very surface or face of life *seems to be*, instead of on that which *is*. Everything of God is hidden to that false sense. This is why it is truly stated that "there is no God in the human picture." None of God is detectable (even though God is fully and tangibly formed all around us) because we are *unaware* of God being all. That of which we are unaware cannot be experienced; only that of which we are *aware* is experienced. Do not forget for even a moment: awareness *is* experience.

When you rest and relax belief from its fixation on sensed formation—the mental, physical and material forms—your rested, relaxed awareness 'makes space' for the silence of God to be felt happening.

"Be still, and know that I [the very I of you, the very consciousness, mind, body and world of you] am God." Still the senses, drop belief, turn within, and begin to feel *presence* happening. Simply detach belief and interest from that which seems to be, to the *real*—spirit itself, the incorporeal, the presence of life itself happening as you, infinity and omnipresence itself happening as the whole of you.

As you practice this you begin to be able to feel your consciousness, your life, your pure presence happening—your 'energy' happening. It doesn't matter how you describe it, or how I do. The important thing is that you become still, withdraw attention and belief from the 'outer' to the 'inner,' and become receptive to the *feeling* of the presence of spirit, truth, God happening as you. "Be still, and know that I am God."

STAND STILL AND SEE

"Stand still and see [feel, witness, experience] the salvation [the truth, health, harmony, peace, oneness, wholeness and completeness] of the Lord which he will show you this day [this very moment]."

Bathe in the presence of God, let the omnipresent light of love and grace flood you and fill you full, illumine all your senses so that you become aware of, and see, and have *conscious tangibility* of this world filled with God, spirit and truth.

Rest, relax, be still, be peaceful, be spacious, be receptive. Be attentively open to God happening as your entire 'you,' and *simply receive.* That's all.

IT IS TIME TO TRULY IGNORE APPEARANCE

From the human standpoint—the human degree of awareness—the kingdom looks somewhat incomplete, out of place, contentious, unhappy, limited, lacking, discordant, diseased, unsafe, insecure, unreliable, variable as well as good, harmonious, healthy, wealthy and fulfilled.

But this standpoint or 'view' of the kingdom is belief about it being its own entity, an existence different from and separated from God, an existence consisting of pairs of opposites, good and bad. It is not *true* seeing or *clear* seeing. "We see through a glass, darkly." Comprehension—'seeing clearly'—is the *only* aspect of being we are dealing with in awakening. Nothing else, nothing different, nothing less.

Awakening is just what it says: *awakening*—becoming 'clear-sighted,' becoming fully *conscious* of that which is, truth rather than untruth. We become *awake* and *clear-seeing.* We awaken to the miracle of God being all, 'happening' in experience as infinite expression, form, quality and amount, right here wherever you are, as you—the spiritual you experiencing its spiritual world and universe.

Our state of conscious awareness—spiritual discernment and comprehension—determines our state of experience. Nothing we see, hear, taste, touch, smell or think *in and of its own self* is comprehension of truth. Rather, if we believe the 'it' we're observing as being an actual entity in and of its own self, we are accepting *concepts* of truth, but never truth itself until we realize that *all is God* despite the way it appears to be. Then, with that, truthful realization, experience begins to, and ever more consistently does, reveal itself as the very experience of harmony, health, abundance, peace, freedom and fulfillment.

Wherever you are this moment, and whatever you discern as 'reality,' the unchanging *truth* is that you stand on, are surrounded by, and are observing and experiencing holy ground—infinity and omnipresence of all that God is and has.

Whatever you see, hear, taste, touch, smell and think is holy ground, the fullness of God in, and as, full manifestation, form and expression, self-complete, whole, perfect, purposeful, joyous and free. Indeed, it is time to truly ignore appearance as the presence, power, amount, character or nature it suggests it is and tries to have you believe it is.

Never judge by the appearance. *Nothing* of appearance, of its own self, is truth. Therefore ignore it.

Nothing that seems to be, is. Therefore nothing that seems to be 'good' is, and nothing that seems to be 'bad' is. Why judge, therefore? Why fret? Why worry? Why fear? Why react? Why make effort to try to fix or pacify or heal or prosper the appearance? Why struggle and strive to either improve the 'bad' things and conditions of appearance or gain more of the 'good?'

Making such effort is where and how we fail as awakening beings. We have not taken literally Jesus' decree to, *Take no thought for your life*—life as it appears to be, the world and all its detail as it appears to be to 'human' comprehension. *Judge not according to the appearance but judge righteous judgement.*

Judge by—sense by, react and respond to, rely on—truth *alone*, God *alone*, the presence and reality of spirit and truth *alone*.

GOD GOVERNMENT

Dismiss appearance. Rest from that which seems to be and immerse yourself in the unconditional love of God consciousness. Close your eyes, turn 'within' to pure consciousness where you are unperturbed by appearance, and ponder—

All is God.

Nothing that exists, exists God-less. Everything that exists is the fullness of God as the form of experience. Nothing is without God, nothing lacks God, or is less than or different from God. All is God and the whole thereof. All is the very presence and mind-form of God itself, infinity and omnipresence itself.

God is, nothing 'else' is. Therefore, all is under the government of God, for there is no other presence, no other operating activity, law, principle or form.

Observe something in your world—any person, thing, amount, activity or condition, good or bad—and realize immediately that what he, she or it appears to be *in and of its own self* is not true, has no reality, no power, no substance, no form, no life, no amount, no quality or ability of its own.

What all *truly* is, is God—infinity and omnipresence. Because only God is, the only thing that ever presents itself to you is God—infinity and omnipresence, not finiteness, local presence or limited form. Only God is, *literally*, therefore only God-*form* is, literally. The only thing you can observe or experience, is the full presence and form of God. God *is* the very form, substance and activity you experience. There is none else.

Now, knowing this truth, practice observing *God*, not just appearance. Realize that all, despite the way in which it appears to be, or act, and despite what collective idea or belief believes it is, is *actually* not only the very presence and form of God, but is fully governed by, and *being* God-form, therefore the form of life, harmony, wholeness, abundance, peace and fulfillment.

Not a grain of whole and fulfilled form is missing or out of place or separate. Not a hair or breath, an atom or cell is out of place. Not a person, thing, amount or condition of absolute fulfillment is separate or apart from this very place or condition you are experiencing. It may and often does *appear to be* incomplete, discordant or lacking in some way but appearance is nothing more than belief and its apparent experience. It is never true or actual.

Omnipresence is this very place, formation and condition you are observing. Omnipresence is the only presence. You are that and everything you observe is that. "I am that I am." Nothing 'else' or 'less' or 'different' is because there is no other substance or quality or presence that a 'different type' of form could be made from. Omnipresence—the whole of God, good, life, love, freedom, completeness, and fulfilled purpose of being (your truthful being) is *actually* the place, form or condition you are observing or experiencing. Nothing you can do or fail to do, and no degree of awareness or unawareness can change that one and only truth. God *is* all, period.

It doesn't matter where you place your awareness, what you are observing or experiencing and how belief would describe its appearing 'reality.' How it appears, acts, and what belief would have you believe about it is not important because it is not real or truthful. Appearance in and of its own self is no more real than believing the characters on the movie screen are real.

What you are *actually* observing and experiencing—which means actually *being*, because all is awareness *being*—is the absolute wholeness and perfection and unadulterated fulfillment of God as all form, therefore of form *governed* by and as God.

ALL 'PARTS' ARE PRESENT, COMPLETE, PERFECT, HERE AND NOW

Nothing is missing from the utter fulfillment of each form, part, place and moment of experience. Each moment of experience is fulfillment experienced because there is none but fulfillment (God). Every observation is fulfillment observed. Each him, her, it, activity, amount, place and condition is fulfillment *happening as experience*, but always *fulfillment* because there is no other 'type' of experience that could happen—just as if we made formations of water, each and every formation is *of* water and cannot possibly be of anything different or less.

It is true that as we look out through the lens of belief, truth—fulfillment—appears not to be so. That is why Jesus admonished, *Judge not according to the appearance.*

That which appears to be as we observe the three-dimensional and five-sensed experience of mind is *in and of its own self* a lie just as the movie picture in and of its own self is deceiving. It is nothing more or less than false imagery *if believed*. If not believed, then all form is 'free' to be its "image and likeness" of God.

Nothing of belief is real! All believed experience is conceptual, opinionated, idealized formation, a false sense, a non-reality. Therefore, why judge what 'is' and what 'is not' by the presentation of belief?

Interestingly, Webster describes *image* as:

1: a reproduction or imitation of the form of a person or thing; especially: an imitation in solid form: statue.

2a: the optical counterpart of an object produced by an optical device (as a lens or mirror) or an electronic device; b: a visual representation of something: as (1): a likeness of an object produced on a photographic material (2): a picture produced on an electronic display (as a television or computer screen).

3: exact likeness : semblance (God created man in his own image—Genesis 1:27)

4a: a tangible or visible representation : incarnation (the image of filial devotion); b archaic: an illusory form : apparition.

5a (1): a mental picture or impression of something (had a negative body image of herself) (2): a mental conception held in common by members of a group and symbolic of a basic attitude and orientation (a disorderly courtroom can seriously tarnish a community's image of justice — Herbert Brownell); b : idea, concept.

6: a vivid or graphic representation or description.

7: figure of speech.

8: a popular conception (as of a person, institution,

or nation) projected especially through the mass media (promoting a corporate image of brotherly love and concern—R. C. Buck)

SUBJECTIVE EXPERIENCE IS NOT TRUTH

Realize, any image, anything we are able to name, is conceptual, conditional, three-dimensional and finite. Therefore it is a *subjective* experience, and if subjective then of either individual or collective *opinion*, never of *reality*.

Friends, stop once and for all judging by appearance— believing it, reacting to it, loving, hating, fearing it, investing and exerting effort to either gain its good or be rid of its bad.

All appearance at its face value is nothing but falsely believed imagery—subjective, conceptual, of idea and belief and never the reality which it truly is. As in observing a movie, we can say the imagery playing before us on the screen is nothing in and of its own self, but is 'false imagery,' a subjective idea or story playing out in front of us as this moment of experience, but never reality itself.

OUR WORK THIS WEEK

Rest your awareness just a blink more deeply than on that which appears to be. Rest back in the unconditionally loving omnipresence of God, spirit, truth, that which is true and real, that which is your truth and reality here and everywhere, wherever you place your awareness, wherever you *are being* at every moment.

Realize that *this very place* "on which you stand" is holy ground, whole and complete being, body, thing, activity, amount and condition—God itself and the "fullness thereof"—under the full government of itself, God, good, life, love, oneness and completeness of joy, harmony, peace and fulfillment of being in every way and as every form.

Rest, rest, rest in the government of God being all you are and all you experience. Then watch how that government reveals all in and as your every moment of experience to be true, lively, loving, plentiful and free.

Think deeply about *all* being the finished kingdom of God, good, and all being governed by that good—life, love, fulfillment of joy, abundance of all thing and circumstance and activity, and unconditionally so, not influenced or affected by anything you do or fail to do, think or fail to think, know or fail to know, anything either 'negative' or 'positive' in appearance or deed.

Think, *think*. Every tiny detail and moment of your experience—without exception, without condition—is governed and complete as the whole of God, good happening as and for your fulfilled and freely-expressing experience and purpose of life.

Ponder these truths deeply, gently, sacredly, for there is no other truth, no other reality, no other world, no other you, no other experience. "I am the only God."

Then *let* the governed experience of truth become, in your sacred silence and receptivity, "a fountain of water springing up into everlasting life"—the experience of all that appears to be lacking and discordant "springing up into a wellspring of" harmonious, healthy, peaceful, happy, wise, abundant and divinely fulfilled being.

Let God *be* God *as* God *for* God as you, 'through' your devotion to truth and your silence of being. In this way you are the 'outlet' of God on earth. You are spiritual presence *as* earth, the "good servant" of truth, and you then only have to *behold* the good and fulfilled formation of God 'happening' as experience.

WEEKS TEN – TWELVE

THE
THIRD
TRUTH

THE THIRD TRUTH

❦

We have come a long way in just nine weeks (nine chapters). If you have been seriously working with and pondering each week's truths, contemplating their profound meanings ever more deeply and more dimensionally, with ever greater texture and flavor—which never ceases becoming *more* and *brand new, fresh formation,* the daily "fresh manna"—your being is already much spiritually nourished, lifted and enriched with greater harmony evident in most or at least some of your world.

The flow of witnessed fruitage is becoming evident as the formation of experience.

THE LITMUS TEST

Witnessing the fruitage of good, God, is the litmus test, the test we give ourselves and by which we live. If God is tangibly evident as our experience, or at least beginning to be in some aspects of experience, then the truth with which we are nourishing ourselves is taking root, pushing through, and becoming the evident "buds, leaves, flowers and fruit" of good and harmonious experience.

Only *tangible evidence* of God in experience is the evidence that we are beginning to live by truthful identity, which is God as all. If there is little or no greater visible, tangible harmony and freedom in our experience, *there is no greater spiritual awareness* or, as yet, there is insufficient *spiritualization of being* to realize God as form—the tangible, 'material' good of experience.

REMEMBER

God is one—one consciousness, one being, one body, one place, one amount, one condition, one experience, one world, one now, one*ness*. God—oneness—*is* mind *is* formation.

There is never 'inner' enriched being or awareness without 'outer' tangible evidence *unless* you entertain the idea of the 'inner' being different from the 'outer' experience—God being different from mind and different from formation (experience). All is God. All is one—all, all, *all!* There is no such thing as an 'inner' versus an 'outer' in actuality. Only in belief does an 'inner' versus an 'outer' exist.

In oneness how can there be two? How can oneness consist of 'two' states of consciousness, 'two' states of embodiment, 'two' states of manifestation, 'two' states of tangibility, 'two' states of visibility— one state '*un*embodied, *un*manifested, *in*tangible and *in*visible' to human sense, while another state is 'embodied, manifest, tangible and visible'?

What would be *happening*, where and to what and for what reason, to prompt the change from intangible to tangible when God *already* is all, one, complete, whole and omnipresent? "The place whereon you stand [your awareness] is holy [whole, omnipresent] ground."

Remember, "The earth [mind-formation] is the Lord's and the fullness [completeness, wholeness, oneness] thereof." God is *already complete, one, manifest, tangible, visible.* We can state it like this: *there is only one state of being— oneness and wholeness.*

It is spiritual *awareness* that 'makes' the oneness and wholeness of being manifest, visible and tangible to, or as, sensed experience. Spiritual awareness *reveals* all form in its truthful state—harmonious, healthy and limitless. Truth does not *become* manifested, visible and tangible 'for' the spiritually aware! No, God does not work for us! God is *finished*, not still under construction. God needs no 'help' to be what God already and forever is. And God certainly does not hear the cries, manipulations and efforts of the selfish-self to have its particular desires of the day or month demonstrated, no matter how well-intentioned those desires may seem to be.

God already and fully *is;* therefore it is the *rising* into the *awareness of that which is*—of *God as all*—which reveals God (good) as experience.

Spiritual consciousness experiences itself as formation—God, good alone. Belief experiences *itself* as formation—materiality, good and bad.

When belief about existence no longer occupies conscious space (awareness), clouding that which is, spiritual being and formation is evident everywhere about.

As we spiritualize awareness, material belief is diluted and dissolved and eventually washes completely out of our senses. Hour-by-hour and day-by-day, as we absorb ourselves in truth messages along with periods of silent listening to *is*, material belief gradually dilutes and spiritual awareness emerges. As each and every degree of increased spiritual awareness is born, *there it is as the forms of experience.* Spiritual awareness 'and' its fruitage are one, not two. Spirit *is* the one universe of itself as all forms of experience. Spirit does not 'produce' or need to 'manifest' or 'demonstrate' anything that 'does not as yet exist.' *All already exists!* "There is no new thing under the sun."[1] It is simply that material belief cannot *see* that which is, while

[1] Ecclesiastes 1:9

spiritual awareness can and does.

IF GREATER HARMONY
IS NOT YET WITNESSED

If greater harmony is not yet evident in your life, the reason why is explained in Chapters 1-9. Go back through them. Search both on the and between the lines. Everything you need to tangibly lift and enrich your experience, including the harmonizing of any discord, is revealed in these wonderful chapters from on high.

Take in each chapter more *deeply*. Live with each more *fully* and more *consistently*. Fall in love with each page, taking it into your heart and with you everywhere. Ponder the miracle of God as life, the miracle of God *being individual life*, inclusive of each moment and form of experience.

Realize the literal oneness of truth—the literal oneness of the 'inner' being the 'outer' and the 'outer' being the 'inner.' No longer accept the false belief of God as spirit and man as matter. No, no! There is *just God being all*, therefore just God being man, woman, mind, body, world and universe; and because God is all, spirit and truth is all.

Forget appearance once and for all. Realize that *all* is God; all is spirit and truth omnipresent—all, all, *all!* — without exception *and* without mental hocus pocus making it so. It all already *is so*. Not even Jesus, Gautama, Shankara, Isaiah, Mohammed, Nanak, Lao Tzu or any other illumined master can influence God or bring about something of good that isn't already present (even though unseen by material belief). In their own words all have told us the same truth, "I can of my own self do nothing. . . .[1] [It is] the Father that dwells in me [that] does the works."[2]

God *is*, already. God is one and oneness. As *this truth* is individually awakened to, it becomes quickly evident as

[1] John 5:30   [2] John 14:10

the one true formation of experience. And because "God saw everything that he had made, and behold, it was very good,"[1] the formation of realized oneness is very good in every way.

Bad formation does not exist in God; discordant, unhappy, diseased, poor, unloving, separate, lacking, limited or incomplete form does not exist in God, therefore does not *actually* exist anywhere at any time. God is one and omnipresent, the *whole* being all and every form, the whole of goodness and harmony being all. No 'other' or 'lesser' experience exists in God consciousness, therefore does not exist anywhere in infinity.

Now you can understand the unwitting absurdity of material belief. A materially-sensing person observes a condition that to him or her is discordant, diseased or lacking; yet the *harmony and wholeness of that very condition* stands right there. Harmony and wholeness always are standing right there (everywhere), but material conviction sees it not—a conviction so deeply imbedded that the believed condition is called 'real.'

There is only one real, and that is God, and God is already perfectly and fully-formed as this world. So use your degree of evidenced God, good, as your one and only measure of spiritual progress. "By their fruits ye shall know them."[2] Of course that is true in oneness. It could be no other way. Therefore, if good, and good more abundant, is not at least becoming evident in your experience, revisit Chapters 1-9. Keep working with them for as long as it takes to start realizing and then witnessing the fruits of your increasing spiritual awareness bursting forth with new and glorious fruit like the vineyard in spring.

That bursting-forth-of-fruits will not be long, my friend, as you keep working with the inspiring messages in these pages, and as you continue to ponder their rich

[1] Genesis 1:31   [2] Matthew 7:20

truths, nourishing your being with the illuminating well-spring of spirit.

Now you are ready to move on.

THE THIRD TRUTH

Our journey until this point has been a preparation for the actual experience of God. It is now time for that experience, time to let "the Lord build the house."[1]

All the 'work' of pondering, contemplating, chewing on and living with truth in our thoughts morning, noon and night—thinking about truth instead of matter, fertilizing, nurturing and developing our spiritual faculties—is not the experience itself but a *preparation* for the experience.

We have to make ready our being so that, as and through spiritual awareness, spiritual (good and harmonious) formation becomes evident.

Without this preparation—the withdrawing of belief and fixation from that which seems to be, to that which is—truth cannot be evident. There is no way for 'unprepared' awareness to be able to evidence the world of truth any more than unprepared, rocky ground can evidence a fruitful orchard.

There has to be the environment of truth—*spiritual awareness* rather than material, physical, earthly awareness—for truth to be evident, just in the same way as there has to be a *clean window* for sunlight to be evident in our home. If the window is dirty or covered, it does not provide the environment in which and through which sunshine can be evident, or more than fractionally evident.

Indeed, there has to be a 'clean' environment of being, a God-aware, peaceful and spacious presence of being for the true (God) formation of the world to be evident.

[1] Psalm 127:1

Belief in and attachment to matter clouds awareness. It is as if a dense fog exists throughout an individual's awareness leaving the world's one true and harmonious formation unclear or unseen, therefore unavailable in experience.

A God-aware (spiritually aware) and centered individual has a clear atmosphere of being, a clear and open consciousness that evidences the formation of itself, the "image and likeness of God." There is nothing clouding or fogging true formation and so harmony is evident. Equally, when a God-aware individual enters the scene previously dominated by material belief (therefore of good and bad experience), the fog quickly clears to reveal true formation. The quick revealing of good (true being and formation) is called a 'miracle' by those unaware of God as all and without opposite.

Realize that the collective world and each individual's version of it is simply belief *experienced as formation.* Belief clouds true and perfect formation, making form appear to consist of the nature, quality, and character of that which is being believed.

The forms of belief seem altogether real to the believer. Why? There is no unformed belief, and so when a person or collective number of persons attaches to the believed forms and—in the mire of that universe of belief—starts making effort to pacify or heal its bad and maintain or multiply its good, reality is lost. A dense fog permeates awareness, and the formation of belief is, *by the believer,* deemed to be reality.

In a nutshell, the above explains the individual and world 'condition' humanity has forever experienced, and for which it has forever struggled for solutions—that of much good, life, love, beauty, happiness and accomplishment *and* much bad, unhappiness, ugliness, injustice, failure, pain, suffering and death.

The solution is this, and it is of *principle*, of *God*, *oneness*, not of fixing humanity and materiality in and of its own self: belief requires a believer or race of believers in which, and as which, to exist. You can see therefore, that as soon as the believer withdraws, all forms of belief equally drop away.

How does a believer withdraw from belief—especially in the mire of continually discordant and demanding conditions? There is one way only—the "strait and narrow way."[1] It is by turning away from that which seems to be, ignoring it no matter how persistently real it seems to be and no matter how pressingly it attempts to demand your attention and solution; and by consciously knowing that God is all, by becoming peaceful and spacious in God awareness, and then by *feeling* God happening within.

Only when we have sufficiently lifted our senses into God, filled or re-filled ourselves full of God awareness, is it possible to be really, really still and empty and silent, and in and as and through that stillness and silence, to feel the gentle presence of God happening as our being, body and world. God felt happening *is* the revealed God formation. The fog has been dissolved and God-formation emerges into plain sight.

The world of truthful being and form already exists everywhere about, but the fog of belief has to dissolve in order for that truthful experience to become visible and tangible—to "open out a way for the imprisoned splendor to escape."[2] But do not confuse *knowing* truth with *experiencing* truth. We can know all the truth ever given to the world and not experience a grain of it. On the other hand, when we have lifted our senses sufficiently *by* knowing truth (reading, listening to or attending truth classes; by contemplating or meditating upon truth), and then be-

[1] Matthew 7:14   [2] "Paracelsus" by Robert Browning

come very, very still and silent and open, we *experience* truth happening. As soon as we *feel* (experience) truth happening, we have truthful vision; the fog of belief has dissolved for this moment and all the forms of truth have become visible and tangible. We find ourselves in possession of our health, our plenty, our harmony and our fulfillment.

We have arrived at the divine state of truth itself being experienced. From that moment we are set free. We never look back. We never again have to manage 'our own' lives. We are under the government of God. Now, instead of these being mere *words* of truth, the truth of the words is *actually experienced.* We have discovered our true identity, our true purpose and our true freedom of being.

God felt happening within is what the Psalmist describes in our third statement:

> *Unless the Lord builds the house, they labor in vain who build it; Unless the Lord guards the city, the watchman stays awake in vain.*[1]

The word "house" in scripture refers to *consciousness* or *being.* Unless God itself is *felt* happening as individual consciousness, individual being—"Unless the Lord builds the house"—then God cannot "build" (be evident as the forms of) your world and everything in it and as it.

All the learning and memorizing of truth and all the thinking you can ever do about truth cannot evidence *one beam or brick* of the true house—your true you and true world. All the learning you can ever apply yourself to, all the intellectualizing, all the knowing of and thinking about even the most beautiful and profound truths cannot evidence a single form of truth itself.

---

[1] Psalm 127:1

TRUTH-THINKING IS NOT TRUTH ITSELF

Do not make the mistake of assuming that truth-thinking (thinking about truth) can evidence truth, whereas non-truth thinking (thinking about matter) cannot. *No thinking*—truthful or non-truthful, even the most beautiful or poetic spiritual thinking—can evidence one cubit of truth itself. "Take no thought for your life. . . .[1] Who among you by taking thought can add one cubit to your stature?"[2]

Do you believe that all this writing I am doing evidences, or is *able* to evidence, a single cubit (embodiment, degree, or measure) of truth itself? No. Ah, but what it *does* do is lift my senses all the way to cloud seven or even eight, at which lifted state I am ready to be taken to cloud nine where heaven is visible and tangible as earth. As I am lifted in truth by this writing (which is really nothing but a printed contemplation on truth), I am prepared (still and peaceful, spacious and receptive) for the experience of truth itself: God felt happening within. This is the "strait and narrow way," and there is no other. "Strait is the gate, and narrow is the way, and few there be that find it."[3]

Thinking about truth, 'spiritualizing' awareness, pondering God and God's world of spirit and truth, filling our minds with the awareness of God as all, lifting our awareness into spirit and truth rather than matter and objectivity *perfectly prepares and readies* us to experience truth. With spiritual preparation and readiness, the purified environment of our being can *feel* God happening; and along with the feeling, the tangible, visible, perfectly manifested forms of life become evident. The feeling *is* the experience and is perfectly evident in whole and harmonious form as long as we do not live with the belief in the 'inner' being different from the 'outer.'

[1] Matthew 6:25   [2] Matthew 6:27   [3] Matthew 7:14

ONLY GOD CAN EVIDENCE GOD

You cannot evidence God; I cannot. Even Jesus, Buddha, Shankara, Moses, Isaiah and Elijah cannot. *Only God can evidence God.*

Think how ludicrous it would be if 'we' could evidence God! It would make us greater than, or at least equal to, God. It would give us a power 'on earth' that God seems not to have (otherwise, presumably, God would already be evident on earth). It would make us necessary assistants in the kingdom of heaven. It would mean 'we' have a role to play 'for' God; in other words, God would not be complete in all ways, especially in the 'human' way, without our particular power or use of mind which is able to manifest God where God is unable to manifest itself, by itself. We would play the role of making God visible and tangible where God is invisible and intangible and incapable of doing the 'manifesting' job himself.

What nonsense! How egoistic and ludicrous is such a proposition! Yet this is what millions of spiritual students the world over obviously believe by their daily attempts to 'demonstrate' and 'manifest' God in their lives, and in the particular form *they want* God demonstrated. Millions, maybe billions, of prayers are sent up to God each day and night of every year, asking for idealized good and gain, relief and freedom with the hope that God will grant those prayers, or at least some them. Millions visualize, meditate, affirm or deny, or even sit in silence, hoping that their efforts will make God tangible in their and their world's affairs.

Realize once and for all: thinking has no truth-power or ability whatsoever. Good or bad, thought has no effect on truth. Only God is; therefore only God can evidence itself. When *God is evidenced*, earth becomes "as it is in heaven."

Understand deeply and thoroughly:

*Only God can evidence itself. . . . Only God can evidence itself.
. . . Only God can evidence itself!*

Therefore, 'you' and 'I' have to be *still* and *silent* and *attentive* to God *felt happening* as the deep within, the pure truth of being and world and all its formation—your and my very being and world, as the one truth, as the *one good*—indivisible, fully manifested and complete existence of all.

Only when we have sufficiently spiritually nourished, nurtured, fertilized and lifted our senses with the truth that *only God is* and that nothing 'else' is—that nothing 'else' is real, nothing 'else' has power, substance, body, form, function, activity, amount, condition or place—are we able to be still and quiet, peaceful and attentive enough to feel *that which is.*

By filling ourselves full of God-awareness, we loosen our grip on that which seems to be, and become sufficiently unworried, fearless and receptive to now experience God as our all-in-all.

ARE 'YOU' THERE?

God is happening as you twenty-four hours a day. But, as the spiritual teacher asked, "Are you there?"

God is individual being inclusive of individual experience. And because God is forever whole and complete, infinite and omnipresent, indivisible and inseparable, *all* of God is what you are and have and what your experience is and has. "You are ever with me, and all that I have is yours."[1]

But because awareness is experience, if we are unaware

[1] Luke 15:31

that "I am ever with you, and all that I have is yours," we do not and cannot experience it.

God is happening as you twenty-four hours day, but are you aware and attentive and receptive to it? If God is not evident in our experience, then, by definition, the answer to "Are you there?" is *No*, we are not there! Before we begin to awaken, we are mostly aware of everything *but* truth! We are mostly aware of what *appears to be*—the mental, material, physical, earthly way in which we sense God. Then, as we stir into some measure of awakened sense, we become a little aware of God but still mostly aware of matter. This stage is hell; the battle is on (but battle not, friend). Gradually, as we fill ourselves full of as much spiritual awareness as we can each day and night, we become ever more aware of God as the only actual reality, with very little remaining material belief in us.

But no matter where we are in our spiritual awakening, God is always fully present and fully *tangibly available.* The way of it? Each time you sufficiently fill yourself with God awareness—'sufficiently' meaning the point at which you feel a sense of *release* from that which troubles you, a feeling of peace about you, a sense of relief that that which seems to be the problem is not real but a falsely-believed problem—you simply become still and silent, and attentive to *God happening as your true being.* As you feel God happening within, you can be assured that the "Lord is building, revealing your house" of experience, and that all will quickly be well.

THE MIRACLE OF TRUTH EXPERIENCED

Nothing else but *this* is the miracle of truth: the *consciously-experienced happening within*, with no effort on your part, no thinking it so, no making it so—just a still and silent openness and receptivity to that which is forever happening as your truth. When that happening is experienced, when you tangibly *feel* a welling-up of peace or harmony or joy or a sense of release or lightness or warmth or freedom from burden, responsibility, and effort, that is when you tangibly *have* God and all the good that God is.

That is the miracle of God as you, *experienced and tangibly evidenced*—the oneness of truth which "bears fruit richly" as harmony, peace, plentiful supply of all good things and freedom in all of experience. *That* is when oneness becomes real in experience, when the 'inner' and the 'outer' experientially merge into the one harmonious reality they truly are.

OUR WORK THIS WEEK

Realize that *only God can evidence God.* Therefore, maintain a nourished and fertile consciousness by continuing to ponder truth. Never cease from consciously realizing the presence and wholeness of truth. Twenty-four hours a day, keep truth alive in your awareness. Keeping truth alive in your awareness is itself the opening and nourishing of being.

Begin also to rest more often throughout the day and night. Be silent more often, listening to the deep silence within. Be ever more attentive to your *spirit* which forever has perfect visibility and tangibility of itself in all forms, forever beholding its (God's) fully manifested and demonstrated formation of experience. Let spirit behold your truthful world *for you* as you give your whole self to God.

Be still, silent, attentive to, and expectant of "the Lord building your house," to truth *being* and revealing itself as your experience. Let consciousness itself *be* everything you are and everything you experience. If you do not let consciousness be itself as you (by daily experiencing God happening within), then all the contemplation and 'knowing' in the universe will be "in vain." You and I cannot build our truth experience. *Only God is;* therefore only God is God experience. Only God evidences itself—builds, reveals, its experience, its finished kingdom as the unconditional, omnipresent and irrepressible good, purpose and freedom of you. Only God evidences *its* health, wealth, harmony, peace and justice as individual being and world. Nothing 'else' can because nothing 'else' is.

The fields of experience are rich and filled with heavenly fruit *when the Lord builds the house*, but barren when knowledge and thought attempt to build it.

The earth is the Lord's and the fullness thereof.

Unless the Lord builds the house, they labor in vain who build it; Unless the Lord guards the city, the watchman stays awake in vain.

THE GOD EXPERIENCE

❧

Nothing but God *felt* or *heard* happening within is God witnessed—God evidenced as formation. If there is no experience of God felt happening within, there is no experience of God happening as its true form because God and God-form are one. "I and the Father are one."

Thinking does not make it so; knowledge about truth does not make it so; manipulating the mental, material or physical does not make it so. Only God is, and only God experienced—God felt happening within—is God *evident* as form (just as we can understand that the sun is evident not by thinking, not by knowledge or by any mental manipulation, but only by experiencing the sun itself, the sun happening).

When God *is* evidenced 'through' the presence of any individual living as sufficient spiritual awareness and stillness and nothingness of personal sense, miracles of true formation and transformation are witnessed on earth.

All the work of knowing truth more deeply and more thoroughly, more vividly, more concretely; all the work of lifting belief and fixation away from the mental, material and physical, away from time and space, process and method, amount and condition, avenue and activity, cause and effect into the awareness of only-God-is, is *preparation* for the experience itself, never itself the experience. It is the spiritualizing of awareness, the cleaning and spiritually purifying of the house (being) in readiness to receive the almighty guest—*the experience of the presence of God itself.*

The senses of being must be unattached and restful in God. We must be still and attentive to spirit, a being of rest and peace, in order to feel the presence of God happening. Belief is the antithesis of spirit, truth, rest and peace; belief is attachment, activity, unrest, anxiety, effort, attainment—the personal sense of being attempting to survive and satisfy itself and its lot. As truth awareness rises in us and we become aware that only God is, we equally become free of belief about experience in and of its own self, thereby free of anxiety about and desire and effort for the objective experience. We become free and fulfilled in spirit, therefore free of that which we call the 'mental, material and physical' belief.

ONENESS—NO 'INNER' VERSUS 'OUTER'

God, therefore *all*, is *one*. There is no 'inner' versus 'outer.' The kingdom of God, oneness, is the *only* kingdom—the *only* and *one* being, body, thing, place, amount, activity, world and universe. How wonderful and freeing to lose the false notion of 'within' versus 'without'! There never has been such division, such difference, such separation.

All is one, all is God, all is omnipresence. Where therefore, could a 'within' versus a 'without' exist? Where in oneness, God, omnipresence does 'two' exist—two of anything, including that duality deemed as 'inner' versus 'outer'?

The more we grasp the truth that that which has been named 'human, mental, material, physical' experience is simply a three-dimensional (objectified) experience of God (of oneness), the more we witness oneness (the truth) *of* experience.

All formation is of mind. Mind *is* formation. Nothing 'else' forms. Form *is* mind; mind *is* form. And because all is God, the Master's statement about "one of the many mansions in my Father's house" is understood to mean one of the infinite degrees of awareness of being, God, oneness. The particular degree of awareness which is 'our' current existence is named the 'human, mental, physical, material, world' degree. This is what 'our mind' is—simply one degree among the infinite degrees of awareness of being, one degree of awareness among the infinity and omnipresence of God.

The more we realize and rest in the truth of oneness, the more the infinity and omnipresence of oneness becomes real and evident as our experience. The perfect spiritual being, body, world and universe exists this minute and forever, experienced *as this very degree of formation we have named 'human' and 'worldly.'* That perfection becomes increasingly real and tangible 'through' the one true consciousness as the fulfillment of every being, condition, activity, amount and place existent as this degree.

You can now see that wherever you place your awareness—anywhere at all throughout this degree of existence, our 'human' and 'this world' degree—*there is the infinity and omnipresence of oneness as all formation.* Why is this true? Oneness, infinity and omnipresence are the only substance, the only presence, the only formation at any and every degree of God awareness.

Forget completely the false idea of 'spirit' versus 'matter,' 'within' versus 'without,' 'God' versus 'humanity,' 'truth' versus 'world.'

> *When you make the two one, and when you make the inner*
> *as the outer and the outer as the inner and the above as*

*the below, and when you make the male and the female
into a single one, so that the male will not be male and the
female not be female. . . then shall you enter the kingdom.*[1]

In using the phrase "enter the kingdom," Jesus refers
to the kingdom of truthful awareness, of God awareness,
of spiritual awareness—of I being God, not human, personal, mental, material or physical, but God, spirit, oneness, allness, infinity and omnipresence. The kingdom of
truth is the kingdom of oneness, the kingdom of consciousness, the kingdom of "I am that I am."

All is *one*—one being, one body, one form, one condition, one activity, one amount, one*ness*, and that *one* is omnipresent, *being* whatever your experience is moment-
by-moment.

All is one; therefore, experience can be, and is, only of
oneness. There is no other substance from which experience can be formed. Indeed, there is no experience other
than that of oneness, *despite a poor degree of awareness of oneness* that any individual or the collective race may be living.

Wherever you place your attention this moment, *there
God is* in all its infinity and omnipresence. And because
God *is* mind *is* form, your mind (the one mind individually experienced as 'yours') is forever full of the goodness
of God which enables you to witness the full goodness of
God as all form—whole and complete, harmonious and
fulfilled, the "image and likeness" of God.

I live and move and have my being in God[2] must be realized
as meaning that I live and move and have my being in the
omnipresence of oneness, *as* omnipresent oneness *itself*
happening as the I that I am.

I live and move and have my being and my entire experience—my entire world and everything everywhere in it
and of it—as the infinite, omnipresent ocean of oneness;

[1] *Gospel of Thomas*, Saying 22   [2] Acts 17:28

and the infinite, omnipresent ocean of oneness lives and moves and has its entire being in and as the I that I am. "I and the Father are one."

If this realization doesn't fill us full of peace and relief and light, and have us rest back from every personal and worldly belief, I do not know what can!

The realization of oneness is critical now, as you make yourself open and receptive to truth and the tangible experience of truth.

All the truth of God being all will not become tangibly evident if you live with a divided belief, an 'inner' versus 'outer' sense of life. This 'divided' belief is one of the major reasons many long-standing spiritual students are not able to evidence the fruits of God in their 'outer' world of form. All the classes they attend, meditation they practice and silence they devote themselves to, and even all the peace they feel happening within as they sit in silence, cannot 'get through' a divided belief—the "divided house" we are warned about in scripture. The peace and wholeness of truth is experienced in their 'within,' yet their 'without' is as devoid of peace and wholeness as it is for the rest of humankind.

Yes! This is so for them because they exist with the belief in a 'within' which is spiritual and a 'without' which is mental, physical and material, a formation which is different from and separate from God, oneness. *If a kingdom be divided against itself, that kingdom cannot stand. And if a house be divided against itself, that house cannot stand.*[1]

The very moment oneness is truly realized and lived in—true oneness and completeness of all being, form, place, activity, amount and condition—then truth becomes ever more evident as the reality of each moment. Truth experienced (felt) happening 'within' *is* truth evidenced 'without' because there isn't an actual within ver-

[1] Mark 3:24-25

sus an actual without; there is just oneness of all, undivided and indivisible.

GOD IS THE ONLY; THEREFORE THE ONLY *EXPERIENCE* IS GOD

The only life, presence, power, body, form, amount and activity is God, spirit, truth. Therefore, the only *experience* is God, spirit, truth. There is none else.

When we feel God happening within, we *have* all of God as all of experience because the 'one' and the 'other' are actually the same *one* presence, the same *one* truth. Anything we call 'experience' is something *felt* or *sensed*—a sensed presence, a conscious awareness, a realized being or object or happening, a consciously sensed moment or activity or condition.

Webster defines 'experience' as—

1a: direct observation of or participation in events as a basis of knowledge, b: the fact or state of having been affected by or gained knowledge through direct observation or participation.
2: practical knowledge, skill, or practice derived from direct observation of or participation in events or in a particular activity.
3: the conscious events that make up an individual life.
4: something personally encountered, undergone, or lived through.
5: the act or process of directly perceiving events or reality.

Nothing but *God experience happening as individual experience* is truthful experience. All 'other' experience is sep-

arate and different from God—false, illusory, vaporous imagery with no law to sustain it, no body or form or activity
or amount or condition of oneness to sustain it. This is
why false experience varies, depletes, lets us down, is unreliable, finite. Nothing we can think, know or do, either
mentally, physically or materially, is truth itself; nor can
bring truth into our experience.

Only God is truth. Only God experience is truthful
experience—the one true, invariable, effortlessly ever-pre-
sent and unconditional good of all experience. Only *God*
experience is unconditional and never separate from us,
always here where we are, now, always fully manifested
and tangible, ours without effort or condition.

Hence, "Unless the Lord build the house they labor
in vain who build it." All the knowing of truth, all the affirming of truth, all the contemplating and meditating
upon truth *is not a grain of truth itself.* Knowing, affirming,
contemplating, meditating—all this is *of the intellect.* It is
the activity of *belief and thought only*, not of truth itself.

All of our learning truth, contemplating and meditating is good and essential *as preparation* for the actual God
experience. We have to get to a state of God-knowing,
stillness and peace, unattached and unconcerned with
that which appears to be. But our preparation is never
truth itself experienced. Indeed, "they labor in vain" who
rely *alone* on truth known, contemplated and meditated
upon.

> Yet, He that believeth on me, as the scripture hath
> said, "Out of his belly [being, consciousness] shall
> flow rivers of living water,"[1] and Whosoever drinks
> of this water [truth known by the intellect alone;
> by mentality, materiality and physicality alone]
> shall thirst again: But whosoever drinks of the water

[1] John 7:38

that I shall give him [God itself felt happening within or as you] shall never thirst; but the water that I shall give him shall be in him a well of water springing up into everlasting life.[1]

The "well of water springing up into everlasting life" is the one omnipresence of God witnessed as all experience—the one being, substance, body, form, amount, freedom and joy of existence. It is God itself experienced as the good that oneness (all) is—as an infinite variety of form and activity, nature and character, opportunity and purpose fulfilled.

Again Jesus instructs us about the one experience: For I say unto you, I will not any more eat thereof, until it be fulfilled in the kingdom of God. And he took the cup, and gave thanks, and said, Take this, and divide it among yourselves: For I say unto you, I will not drink of the fruit of the vine, until the kingdom of God shall come. And he took bread, and gave thanks, and brake it, and gave unto them, saying, This is my body which is given for you: this do in remembrance of me.[2]

Oh! If everyone could understand this profound statement of the Master! "I will not drink of the fruit of the vine, until the kingdom of God shall come." The entire secret of awakened self is contained in these seventeen words. "I will not [I am unable to] drink of the fruit of the vine [because there isn't yet any truthful fruit] until the kingdom of God shall come [shall be *felt happening as individual being and quickly witnessed as form*]."

There it is, the whole secret! This is the secret of unconditional life and happiness, good and harmony, plenty

[1] John 4:13-14   [2] Luke 22:16-19

and fulfillment. It is the secret of the miracle of God itself experienced as tangible form—"heaven as it is on earth."

God felt happening *is itself* your health or healing, your strength and vitality, your beauty and youthfulness, your wealth in every form including dollars, your love and relationship, your peace and harmony, your talent and ability, your wisdom and knowledge—all without condition or opposite.

It is all *one*, yet experienced as 'all'—the multitude of experience. And that oneness comes 'through' into and as experience by being *felt* or *sensed within* as peace or harmony or joy or bliss or ecstasy or freedom or release or relief from the world, or light or warmth or even a deep and beautiful heat.

It can also be *heard* (either audibly or as a feeling or sense) as a truth clarity, instruction, direction or "Aha!" It can be felt as the gentlest and most subtle presence of love assuring you that all is well, and safe. It can be the remembrance or revelation of a beautiful truth statement springing up within.

"The kingdom come" can be experienced in any way and as any form. The important thing to understand is that the God experience—God felt happening in one way or another—is the only *evident truth*, the only actual truth experienced or demonstrated, the only actual experience of God, the only miracle of health, wealth, harmony and peace on earth that the whole world can see and become freed by.

The tangibility and visibility of God as form is infallible as one experiences God itself happening because God *is mind is form;* God is *one* presence, not two. As we experience God happening—as long as we are not the 'house divided' (the awareness unable to see that which is)—good *forms* of God are infallibly ours to see and to freely benefit from.

THE ONE TRUTH CONSCIOUSLY EXPERIENCED

There is no life in your universe but the one life. There is no being, body, activity, amount or condition in your universe but the one. However, this fact does you little tangible good until first, you become aware of it, and second, you let the experience of oneness itself—God itself—be your primary and most important aspect of daily experience.

As you make God-felt-happening your primary and most treasured daily activity, then the "life more abundant" becomes visible and real as your experience. *I am come that you may have life, and that you may have it more abundantly.*[1]

As you *feel* the God experience happening within—the "I am," the kingdom of God coming—you can be assured of your tangible wholeness, your transformed and renewed health and your new immunity to the world's contagions, illnesses, diseases and accidents. You can be assured of your tangible wealth and success, your safety and security, your love and happiness. But you must live by *feeling* God happening as you and your entire world and universe. Living devoid of God felt happening is living devoid of God form experienced—or experience-*able*. God *is* the substance, presence, activity and form; therefore, devoid of the God experience, we make ourselves devoid of the substance, presence, activity and form of God—devoid of the miracle of God as our very life and expression and all its resources and fulfillment. God is this! So let us *experience* God!

[1] John 10:10

YOUR ONLY NEED IS GOD
TANGIBLY EXPERIENCED

If you are lacking what is named 'health,' do not be deceived. The body is the one body forever whole, perfect, vital and free in form. What you are 'lacking' if your body is ill or diseased is God consciously felt as your body. There is nothing else wrong with your body but a lack of *God consciously experienced.*

Therefore, after all your truth knowing, contemplating and meditating, "Stand still and see [experience, feel happening] the salvation of the Lord, which he will show to you this day [be evident as healthy and healed form this day]."[1]

Be still, silent, open, receptive and patiently "wait upon the Lord." Wait for the very omnipresence of life itself to be felt happening within you and flooding your every part, for "Evildoers [those of material belief] shall be [are] cut off [unable to evidence that which is true]: but those that wait upon the Lord, they shall inherit the earth [the true body of experience]."[2]

And "They that wait upon the Lord shall renew their strength; they shall mount up with wings as eagles; they shall run, and not be weary; and they shall walk, and not faint."[3]

The Book of Isaiah describes the emptiness, pain and suffering experienced by the individual who believes in matter, and also the abundance, ability, strength, glory and freedom of being when it is imbued and fulfilled with the experience of God felt happening.

Here are a few more verses of Isaiah, Chapter 40. Read them with spiritual discernment, the understanding that only God consciously felt happening is truth experienced, truth 'achieved,' the actual *awakened, illumined and freed*

[1] Exodus 14:13   [2] Psalm 37:9   [3] Isaiah 40:31

state of being experienced:

1Comfort ye, comfort ye my people, saith your God.

3The voice of him that crieth in the wilderness, Prepare ye the way of the Lord, make straight in the desert a highway for our God.

4Every valley shall be exalted, and every mountain and hill shall be made low: and the crooked shall be made straight, and the rough places plain:

5And the glory of the Lord shall be revealed, and all flesh shall see it together: for the mouth of the Lord hath spoken it.

6All flesh is grass, and all the goodliness thereof is as the flower of the field:

7The grass withereth, the flower fadeth: because the spirit of the Lord bloweth upon it: surely the people is grass.

8The grass withereth, the flower fadeth: but the word of our God shall stand forever.

9O Zion, that bringest good tidings, get thee up into the high mountain; O Jerusalem, that bringest good tidings, lift up thy voice with strength; lift it up, be not afraid; say unto the cities of Judah, Behold your God!

10Behold, the Lord God will come with strong hand, and his arm shall rule for him: behold, his reward is with him, and his work before him.

11He shall feed his flock like a shepherd: he shall gather the lambs with his arm, and carry them in his bosom, and shall gently lead those that are with young.

12Who hath measured the waters in the hollow of his hand, and meted out heaven with the span, and comprehended the dust of the earth in a measure, and weighed the mountains in scales, and the hills in a balance?

13Who hath directed the Spirit of the Lord, or being his counsellor hath taught him?

14With whom took he counsel, and who instructed him, and taught him in the path of judgment, and taught him knowledge, and shewed to him the way of understanding?

15Behold, the nations are as a drop of a bucket, and are counted as the small dust of the balance: behold, he taketh up the isles as a very little thing.

16And Lebanon is not sufficient to burn, nor the beasts thereof sufficient for a burnt offering.

17All nations before him are as nothing; and they are counted to him less than nothing, and vanity.

18To whom then will ye liken God? Or what likeness will ye compare unto him?

19The workman melteth a graven image, and the goldsmith spreadeth it over with gold, and casteth silver chains.

20He that is so impoverished that he hath no oblation chooseth a tree that will not rot; he seeketh unto him a cunning workman to prepare a graven image, that shall not be moved.

21Have ye not known? Have ye not heard? Hath it not been told you from the beginning? Have ye not understood from the foundations of the earth?

22It is he that sitteth upon the circle of the earth, and the inhabitants thereof are as grasshoppers; that stretcheth out the heavens as a curtain, and spreadeth them out as a tent to dwell in:

23That bringeth the princes to nothing; he maketh the judges of the earth as vanity.

24Yea, they shall not be planted; yea, they shall not be sown: yea, their stock shall not take root in the earth: and he shall also blow upon them, and they shall wither, and the whirlwind shall take them away as stubble.

25To whom then will ye liken me, or shall I be equal? saith the holy one.

26Lift up your eyes on high, and behold who hath created these things, that bringeth out their host by number: he calleth them all by names by the greatness of his might, for that he is strong in power. Not one faileth.

28Hast thou not known? Hast thou not heard, that the everlasting God, the Lord, the creator of the ends of the earth, fainteth not, neither is weary? There is no searching of his understanding.

29He giveth power to the faint; and to them that have no might he increaseth strength.

30Even the youths shall faint and be weary, and the young men shall utterly fall:

31But they that wait upon the Lord shall renew their strength; they shall mount up with wings as eagles; they shall run, and not be weary; and they shall walk, and not faint.

Do not these verses speak to you of the whole world of material 'good and bad,' of finiteness, struggle, discord, disease, poverty, famine, cruelty, injustice, unhappiness, impossibility *and* of the entire secret of truth evidenced as individual being and as all those who "wait upon the Lord"?

We could have a whole series of classes on this one chapter of Isaiah. Maybe one day we will. Never will truth be clearer and more tangibly evident than from the day we truly understand what Isaiah is sharing with us, and from the moment we continually *live* truth which means living the actual, tangible experience of God felt happening within as our *one and only* reality and reliance, our *one and only* resource, our one and only true everything everywhere.

EVERY PROPHET TELLS US THE SECRET

I am the way, the truth, and the life.[1]

To this end was I born and for this cause came I into the world, that I should bear witness unto the truth.[2]

Christ [spirit, truth, consciousness] shall give thee light.[3]

Christ is all, and in all.[4]

He [truth experienced within] dispels darkness [material belief, limitation, discord, disease, poverty] by the light of truth and delivers [reveals the truth of] them who through fear and death were all their lifetime subject to bondage.[5]

He is before all things, and by him all things consist.[6]

In him is life, and the life is the light of men.[7]

I am the light of the world; he that follows me [knows and tangibly experiences truth happening within] shall not walk in darkness, but shall have the light of life.[8]

[1]John 14:6   [2]John 18:37   [3]Ephesians. 5:15   [4]Col. 3:11
[5]Heb. 2:15   [6]Col 1:17   [7]John 1:4   [8]John 8:12

I am the bread of life; he that comes to me shall never hunger, and he that believes on me shall never thirst.[1]

Every one that is of truth hears my voice [consciously experiences and relies on nothing but God felt happening].[2]

He that abides in me, and I in him, the same brings forth much fruit.[3]

Without me ye can do nothing.[4]

Come unto me [your truth happening within] all ye that labor and are heavy laden, and I will give you rest. Take my yoke upon you, and learn of me . . . and ye shall find rest unto your souls. For my yoke is easy and my burden is light.[5]

Peace I leave with you, my peace I give unto you: not as the world gives, give I unto you. Let not your heart be troubled, neither let it be afraid.[6]

Ye shall receive power after the holy ghost [truth] is come upon you [is consciously experienced].[7]

When he, the Spirit of truth, is come, he will guide you into all truth.[8]

The Comforter [truth experienced], even the Holy Spirit . . . he shall teach you all things.[9]

I will put my spirit in you, and you shall live.[10]

[1] John 6:35   [2] John 18:37   [3] John 15:5   [4] John 15:5   [5] Matt 11:28-30
[6] John 14:27   [7] Acts 1:8   [8] John 16:13   [9] John 14:26   [10] Ezekiel 37:14

Know ye not that you are the temple of God [God fully and perfectly formed], and that the Spirit [life, experience, actuality, tangibility] of God dwells in you?[1]

Where the Spirit of the Lord is [where the experience of God felt happening within is taking place as individual being], there is liberty.[2]

It is not ye that speak [live, experience truth, be truthful), but the spirit of your Father [the experience of truth itself forever expressing as you] which speaks in you.[3]

It is the spirit that bears witness, because the spirit is [the only] truth.[4]

Not by might, nor by power, but by my spirit, saith the Lord of hosts.[5]

It is the Spirit that quickens [illumines being, evidences truthful life and body], the flesh [the mental, physical, material in and of its own self] profits nothing.[6]

Now we have received, not the spirit of the world, but the Spirit which is of God; that we might know [tangibly experience] the things that are freely given us of God.[7]

OUR WORK THIS WEEK

Our work is not 'ours' but God's—truth's.
Rest, turn within, be still, attentive and receptive, and

---

[1] 1 Cor 3:16   [2] 2 Cor 3:17   [3] Matt 10:20   [4] 1 John 5:7
[5] Zech 4:6   [6] John 6:63   [7] 1 Cor 2:12

be patient while you "wait on the Lord."

Wait until you achieve sufficient stillness, silence and receptivity—seeking the experience of God for *its sake alone*, not for any reason of 'yours' or the 'world's'—until you *feel God happening, welling-up, stirring within.*

This is our daily work this week—being still enough, silent enough, attentive enough so that that which is happening as itself twenty-four hours a day as you can be *felt happening.*

That alone is the miracle of you. That alone is truth evidenced. That alone is the 'healing,' the revealing of truthful being, body, thing, amount, activity, place, condition, world and universe in perfect formation here and now.

Let us devote ourselves more and more consistently to God, to truth, to spirit, thereby revealing all being as divine, all things, activities and amounts as one and infinite, all of this world as heaven, the omnipresence of God, good with "none else."

Only by this way of living—*being*—are we awake and truthful to truth.

Only by this way of being can we evidence the presence of God, good, as all being and formation.

Only in this way can we say that we truly love God and God's formation that we name 'earth.'

LIVING AS AWAKENED BEING

❦

Be not afraid nor dismayed by reason of this great multitude; for the battle is not yours, but God's.[1]

And he arose, and rebuked the wind, and said unto the sea, Peace, be still. And the wind ceased, and there was a great calm.[2]

And he will love thee, and bless thee, and multiply thee: he will also bless the fruit of thy womb, and the fruit of thy land, thy corn, and thy wine, and thine oil, the increase of thy cattle, and the flocks of thy sheep, in the land which he swore unto thy fathers to give thee.[3]

Give, and it shall be given unto you; good measure, pressed down, and shaken together, and running over, shall men give into your bosom. For with the same measure that ye mete withal it shall be measured to you again.[4]

PART ONE

As we arrive at the wondrous state of *only-God-is* awareness—only omnipresence is, only allness, self-inclusive,

[1] 2 Chron 20:15   [2] Mark 4:39   [3] Deuteronomy 7:1   [4] Luke 6:38

self-contained oneness is—we have just one true purpose: to let "the Lord build the house," to let the kingdom of God be visible and tangible as our being and work, whatever that work may be.

We no longer believe, attach to, have concern or fear about, or make effort for either of the pairs of opposites. The "great multitudes" of formed experience are, in and of their own selves nothing but imagery, and we know it.

We know their literal non-substance, non-entity, non-power, non-law or principle, therefore their inability to effect us *in and of their own selves.* We know that belief in them is the only power we give them in our experience, and that even that is a pseudo-power—a believed power appearing to be real.

We understand that only God itself can "build the house" of our mind, body and world because only God is, and we understand that only *God felt happening* is God "building the house."

We are told in scripture to, "Be not afraid nor dismayed by reason of this great multitude; for the battle is not yours, but God's" and we understand why. We make our own battles by believing that which seems to be, satisfied with its good while battling its bad. Both the satisfaction and the battle with that which seems to be is false sense with no God in it (of its own self) whatsoever.

But, a little more awake and alight in truth, we are aware that all appearance is nothing in and of its own self, and that God alone is the power and presence that dissolves the fog of false sense, revealing truthful sense and its "image and likeness" form. Indeed, "the battle is not yours, but God's."

We as a human sense of being have no power, therefore *no ability* of our own. This is very important to realize. We have no ability to illumine our senses or dissolve the fog of false belief. "I can of my own self do nothing." Only God is power; therefore *only God is ability.* Without ability, how can we "build the house"? How can we fill ourselves with spirit or reveal truth where falsity seems to be? What substance or knowledge or materials do we possess in and of our personal sense with which to build a truthful awareness, to illumine the senses, to reveal God on earth? None at all. "My thoughts are not your thoughts; neither are your ways my ways. . . .[1] I am the Lord, and there is none else, there is no God besides me."[2]

And so we rest our senses. We settle down peacefully, receptive, relaxed, still; we become silent and receptive, relinquishing our entire sense and opening our being to God itself. We make of ourselves a vessel for God, empty of thought and effort, silent, open and willing for God to *be* God *as* God *for* God as what appears to be us.

No matter what forms of good or bad face us, we become still and receptive to God, remembering "Be not afraid nor dismayed by reason of this great multitude; for the battle is not yours, but God's."[3]

In and as that rest, that experience of presence or peace or warmth or light and love, the fog of false sense dissolves and all is revealed as good, whole and harmonious. The God of all form is now visible and tangible. It has stood there eternally but now we *see it*, and all is well. The 'healing' has taken place.

PART TWO

"And he arose, and rebuked the wind, and said unto the sea, Peace, be still. And the wind ceased, and there was a great calm."[1]

The disciple Mark is describing a *spiritual* account, not just an historical or material event. "He arose" means *he*

[1] Isaiah 55:8   [2] Isaiah 45:5   [3] 2 Chron 20:15

lifted his awareness to that which is, he *realized truth,* he *raised his senses* to pure truth. He ignored appearance in the knowledge of its nothingness, and acknowledged the *one* power and presence of God—a power not in opposition with another, but the *only.* "He arose" is our *laboring in the fields*—reminding ourselves of truth, contemplating and meditating upon God, oneness, spirit being the only, in order to again lift our awareness into an illumined (spiritual) state.

Then he "rebuked the wind." He looked upon the appearing discord and *knew the truth that only God is; therefore only peace is.*

Webster defines "rebuke" as:

1a: to criticize sharply : reprimand.

1b: to serve as a rebuke to.

2: to turn back or keep down : check.

3: an expression of strong disapproval: reprimand.

We can interpret: to sharply know the nothingness of discord and the allness of God; to "reprimand" the untruthful appearance; to "check" it; to "strongly disapprove" of it, or "strongly ignore" it in the certainty that nothing but God exists.

Then "he said unto the sea [the senses], Peace, be still." He "told" his senses to be peaceful and still rather than accepting a collective belief of disarray. His senses became filled with peace and stillness, light and love, harmony and calm.

He demanded that truth alone be his formed experience, his tangible environment and atmosphere.

"And the wind ceased, and there was a great calm." The formed environment around us infallibly reveals itself to be the "image and likeness" of God—harmonious and peaceful—*when oneness is on the scene.* "Where the spirit of the Lord [oneness] is, there is liberty."[2]

[1] Mark 4:39   [2] 2 Cor 3:17

The "spirit of the Lord" is *God experienced happening* 'within' or as individual being. *That* is "the Lord building the house"—God becoming evident *as itself*, as the "image and likeness" of itself 'happening' as individual being—even happening as the ocean's calming down, which a minute ago was frighteningly stormy.

Jesus was so completely filled with the light of truth that no 'mental or physical Jesus' was left in his awareness. His very presence was that of God, not matter, not objectivity, not corporeality or physicality. His was the consciousness, mind and body of infinity and omnipresence.

God-presence pacifies and harmonizes everything in its atmosphere that seems, to material belief, to be stormy, disharmonious or discordant, and so in the Master's presence "the wind ceased, and there was a great calm." The disciples were amazed, "saying one to another, What manner of man is this, that even the wind and the sea obey him?" They had not yet grasped the truth of spiritual identity and so they asked the wrong question. There was no "manner of man" about the Master, only the manner of God—the very presence of God as individual being, God on earth, "heaven as it is on earth."

THE MANNER OF MAN

The "manner of man" which all formation "obeys" is the *spiritual man*, the illumined consciousness of oneness, the truth of man, woman and universe being spiritual, not material. Existence does not contain God *and* man, God *and* world and everything in it. Existence *is* God alone. God *is* all, God *is* one, and that allness and oneness is *spirit* without any matter in it whatsoever.

There is none but God—spirit. This leaves no space, place or formation for anything but God or made of anything but God. What we have named *being* or *life* is God, what we have named *mind* is God, and what we have named *formation [earth and universe]* is God. "The earth [all formation, all of experience, all which can be named] is the Lord's and the fullness thereof."[1]

This means that the only identity in existence is God—spirit and truth—not God *and* matter; not God *and* human, animal, vegetable, object, amount, activity, place and condition. The only identity is spirit, the wholeness and goodness of God itself. Nothing less, different, separate or temporary exists. Existence itself is all that exists—the *only*, the *whole* of existence existing at each point and place of itself simultaneously. This truth is what every spiritual teacher and teaching reveals.

If the disciples had understood truthful identity they would not have asked, "What manner of man is this, that even the wind and the sea obey him?" Instead, they would have simply—with great humility and silent awe—observed the truth and glory of God *as individual spiritual consciousness* dissolve all discordant appearance. They would also have understood another great truth their Master revealed—that "the works you see me do, you can do also, and greater than these you can do."[2] The Master was teaching them that all beings are the same *one* being: God and none other—"my Father and your Father; my God and your God,"[3] the one Father (truth) of all beings and things, earth and universe.

God, which is consciousness, *is* the infinity and omnipresence of existence—the *one* substance, mind and formation of all life.

"He that sees me sees him that sent me."[4] All is God, spirit, truth. All is! All is! *All is!* Therefore, when you observe any person, thing, amount, activity, condition or place, it is God *actually*—"the Father [truth]"—despite the

---

[1] Psalm 24:1; 1 Cor 10:26   [2] John 14:12   [3] John 20:17   [4] John 12:45

way it appears to be, appears to act, how 'much' it appears to be or consist of, its condition or place or purpose, its apparent positive and constructive or negative and destructive disposition.

NOTHING BUT GOD EXISTS

The appearance in and of its own self is one hundred percent illusory, either good or bad—or better said, *neither* good nor bad. It is God alone, for nothing but God exists, and no other quality or condition but the omnipresence of God exists.

Spiritually illumined awareness knows this and is therefore, undisturbed by and uninterested in appearance in and of its own self. Illumined awareness knows what truly is—the truth which is hidden from 'human' perception by the foggy mask of material belief. It knows that the truth of all is God itself, pure harmony, freedom, joy and fulfilling purpose of being and world.

Illumination reveals that the infinity of God is omnipresent as all form, and this enables every illumined individual to live freely and purposefully with the unconditional infinity of all resource ever at hand. Limitless supply of all formation is instantaneously available as real and tangible experience when truth is known and lived, when appearance never fools us and *God itself* is the only experience sought. *Then* it is that God—through and as God consciousness (God as mind as formation)—reveals its perfect, plentiful, whole and harmonious "image and likeness" as experience.

FREE IN GOD AS EARTH

Wherever attention is placed, that 'place' is God experienced. When we know that, we are free in God as earth and its every rich resource; when we do not know it and are still fixated with the belief in appearance being something separate or different from God, we are imprisoned by the pairs of opposites we ourselves are being; and we have to live in our prison and manage it as best we can, until we set ourselves free (in the very way described in this book). "Know the truth, and that very truth will set you free."[1]

"Where the spirit of the Lord is [where the presence of spiritual consciousness is], there is liberty."[2] Liberty *is spiritual consciousness,* which is one as (appears as) its formation of experience. Spiritual or God consciousness *is itself* liberty 'from' all material ties and bondage, limitation and lack, pain and suffering. Spiritual consciousness does not have matter in it, therefore does not have the pairs of opposites that material belief is. Spiritual consciousness does not have ties and bondage, limitation and lack, pain and suffering; it has only itself. And because of this, it simply beholds all manner of limitation and discord melt to reveal truthful, whole and harmonious form—the *one* truthful and ever-existent form now evident and real to experience.

The more you know the truth and ignore appearance—accepting it as just appearance, not reality, not power, not any kind of body, function, amount, activity, character or condition of its own self, *remaining in, and being God consciousness*—the more you witness "the wind and the sea obey him [you]." The storms of life, the discord and disease, lack and limitation, pain and suffering of life "obey" your spiritual consciousness, and are dissolved to reveal truthful (whole and harmonious) mind, body and condition.

[1] John 8:32   [2] 2 Cor 3:27

PART THREE

"And he will love thee, and bless thee, and multiply thee: he will also bless the fruit of thy womb, and the fruit of thy land, thy grain, and thy wine, and thine oil, the increase of thy cattle, and the flocks of thy sheep, in the land which he swore unto thy fathers to give thee."[1]

As we finally recognize—literally and tangibly—that only God is, that nothing 'else' is, therefore as our entire awareness, our thoughts and contemplation, our desire and our effort are only and continually to know more of God, to be "taught of God,"[2] and to behold God as the free-flowing and freely unfolding formation of our experience (rather than make effort for experience), we have discovered the greatest secret of harmonious, whole and purposeful life.

Our one and true purpose is to discover truth and live it, to reveal the glory of God as individual and collective being and experience. When we have God consciousness, we have all that God is, and we are able to live the free and purposeful life we are meant to live right here on earth— "earth as it is in heaven."[3]

We have discovered that true life and everything of it is God and is finished, whole and perfect, purposeful and free, and instantaneously available as omnipresent good for all.

We discover that the limitlessness of being becomes real and tangible as experience. Awareness opens to that which is—awareness moves, expands and blossoms *seeing* and *having* ever more of that which is. Magnifying *awareness* experiences more of the infinity and omnipresence of God, already and forever formed and whole, never incomplete, lacking, limited or discordant.

We discover that infinity—omnipresence, omnipotence

---

[1] Deuteronomy 7:13   [2] John 6:45   [3] Matthew 6:10

and omniscience—is the reality of not just God-being, but God *as individual being.* "I am that I am."[1] We discover that our true (always individual and unique) purpose here on earth is to *reveal* God as all, reveal *oneness and unity* as all and for all without condition, without creed, without judgment or demand.

We discover that the world and its people, things, amounts and conditions give freely and voluntarily of their good, their love, their substance and form, as a flower freely gives of her delicacy, beauty, color, and fragrance. We discover that God is evident as and through all being and things, places and conditions, activities and amounts. We witness God *as* and *being* all. God—fulfillment—meets us at each and every step, every move, every place, every opportunity and activity, and indeed *is itself* the very body, function and formation of all we are and all we meet. "In [and as] God we live, and move, and have our being."[2]

The spiritually-recognized and -realized earth opens and gives all of herself to the spiritually-identified and -living individual. Why? That we can do the only thing that spirit does—ceaselessly, freely and unconditionally *give to* and *serve* our world of neighbors, colleagues, friends, customers, patients, students, strangers, places and conditions.

When you live your spiritual identity, all of the earth—human, animal, plant, vegetable, object, activity, amount and opportunity—recognizes you and offers its good to you and yours. All the beauty and bounty, harmony and joy, infinity and omnipresence, knowledge and wisdom of divine being opens its doors, invites you in, and lavishes you with its good *because it knows you as it knows itself*—as *spiritual* being with *spiritual* purpose.

Indeed "He will love thee, and bless thee, and multiply thee: he will also bless the fruit of thy womb, and the fruit of thy land, thy grain, and thy wine, and thine oil, the in-

[1] Exodus 3:14   [2] Acts 17:28

crease of thy cattle, and the flocks of thy sheep, in the land which he swore unto thy fathers to give thee."

Your being—all-inclusive of the earth and everything she is and has—is ever full to overflowing, fulfilled, consummated and unconditionally available at your every step *when* you know your truth and let God live it.

Our truthful purpose is now clear and one-pointed: to give, serve and share of our infinity and divinity of being in all ways and of all things.

PART FOUR

"Give, and it shall be given unto you; good measure, pressed down, and shaken together, and running over, shall men give into your bosom. For with the same measure that ye mete withal it shall be measured to you again."[1]

In the spring of 2011 it was revealed to me that *after all is said and done, the only human malady is a lack of giving.* As we awaken to the truth that the whole of God—the *whole,* the infinitude itself, existing at every point of consciousness simultaneously—is embodied in and as, and is fully *being,* individual consciousness (the kingdom of God within you), then we realize there is just *one way* in which to tangibly witness the infinity of being and earth: *to freely give of it.*

Nothing of God can be gained, earned, won or forced. Nothing of God can be added or taken away because God is already and invariably the omnipresence of itself as you, me and all.

All is within, and that 'all' is consciousness, God, spirit, fully embodied in and as, and being your, my and all persons' individual consciousness. Nothing can change that truth, lessen it, dilute it, make it different or separate it from who and what we are. But the knowledge of this

[1] Luke 6:38

truth alone does us no good. We cannot witness a single grain of God until we are *being* God being instead of 'human' being. To witness the one consciousness as all form—the so-called intangible, transcendental, incorporeal, the kingdom of heaven and its treasures on earth—we have to *be* and *give it, pour it out, release it.*

Imagine the sun failing to give of its being, failing to pour out its substance, its light and heat? There would be no confusion about why its experience—its universe—was lacking and limited in light and heat.

Imagine the sun's confusion if, witnessing a lack and limited amount light and heat in its universe, it attempted to borrow from other suns? Imagine its confusion if it attempted to gain or earn or win light and heat from *outside of itself,* by employing outside help, vehicles, avenues or methods—or by any means other than that of *releasing the infinity of its own being,* the infinity of all the light and heat it *is* and *has,* that *only it itself* is and has, and only it itself can pour out to witness.

Of course, it is only as the sun *pours out* that which it *is* and *has* that, first, it becomes visible and tangible in the universe and, second, endlessly *more of it* becomes visible and tangible. Only as it ceaselessly gives of its substance and every form thereof is its good form 'multiplied,' more abundantly evident in "good measure, pressed down, shaken together, running over."

The more water a hose pours forth, the more is made visible and tangible—the more abundance of water is evident in the hose's world.

As soon as we awaken to the truth of being—the spiritual identity and infinity of being and world—we realize the same 'giving' principle applies to us. We must give of ourselves in order to witness our wholeness, harmony and happiness of life. If we do not know the truth and then do not get busy giving and sharing in every way we can, our good remains locked up inside of us and invisible to experience. It isn't present in experience if we do not *give it to experience.*

Life must consist of *outflow* not *inflow.* The more we attempt to 'get' from life, the more we live in the dark of human and material belief with all its apparent lack and limitation, discord and disease, pain and suffering. But the more we know the truth and then *give, pour out, express, share, serve,* the more of the miracle of infinity and unconditional harmony is evident as our experience.

OMNIPRESENT OUTFLOW

Because of oneness—omnipresence—the outflow of you can and does appear from anywhere and everywhere in your kingdom, your earth.

Unlike the sun and hose metaphors, which pour forth and evidence their substance and form from within their physical selves to the physical outer, oneness pours forth *from all over itself simultaneously* and *gives back* from all over itself simultaneously. In God, in omnipresence, 'giving' and 'receiving' is one and the same action. And more than one act, giving forever multiplies the good of experience, revealing ever more of infinity, of omnipresence as all being and form. Oneness, omnipresence, cannot perform in any other way.

Think! There would have to be 'twoness' in order for there to be giving 'from' within 'to' the without which then 'receives' that which is given. 'Giving' would have to be an expression from a giving place somewhere in God, to a receiving place which is somewhere different in God. This idea is not of oneness, but twoness. There would have to be two activities, a giving cause and a receiving effect. This cannot be and is not true or possible in God, oneness, omnipresence. And because God is all, it is neither true nor possible in *experience*.

LET US UNDERSTAND

All is one—*one* being, one mind and one experience, oneness. Oneness (omnipresence) does not have a 'cause' department versus an 'effect' department. Oneness and omnipresence are what they claim to be: *one being all*, all being the *whole* of oneness without anything missing or lacking or separate or different or less. No place of oneness 'needs more' of itself in order to become whole and complete.

No! Oneness is already the *whole* of itself, and omnipresence is already the *whole* of presence. There isn't any 'more' of oneness or omnipresence to get or have or give or receive.

Not only is oneness and omnipresence all and one, but *is itself* the very body and activity, substance and form of all. When you observe any him, her or it, you are observing oneness and omnipresence—the whole of God. If you believe the appearance, you won't see this truth, you will see only the formation of your belief.

But if you know you are observing God, therefore paying little attention or interest to the being or form in and of its own self and let God itself reveal to you the truth of what you're observing, you will experience God, and the nature and quality of God.

BRING THE MULTITUDES INTO ONE

Bring the multitudes of experience into *oneness*. Bring all busyness and noise, all activity and effort, all names, conditions, characters, amounts and places, all good and all bad back *here*, home in oneness. Unplug the power of the "ten thousand things,"[1] the efforts and noisy multiplicity of experience—including the whole of cause and effect and time and space in which all experience seems to exist. Release it and let it go for *oneness*, God. Then rest, and let truth reveal the oneness and harmony, wholeness and completeness of all.

Know the truth, then rest, and behold God becoming real and visible as your world as the fog of false belief dissolves. "Stand still, and see the salvation of the Lord, which he will show to you this day."[2]

NO CAUSE, NO EFFECT, JUST ONENESS

Tell me, in the omnipresence of oneness, where could there exist a *cause* which triggers a different existence named an *effect?* Where would or could there exist a *giving inner* that triggers a *giving back outer?*

Of course, there could not. All is one, whole and complete existence—one substance, one presence, one body, one activity, one experience, always consisting of the whole at each point or place of itself simultaneously. Because the *whole* is omnipresent, no point or place or body or activity exists in lack of wholeness, limited or discordant in some way, unhappy or unfulfilled, left needing 'more' life or substance or quality or form to fulfill it.

Ah, but you say God is different from world experience. No! All is God, all is oneness, all is omnipresence, all is whole and complete! Experience is different *only if we believe it to be.* Belief separates us from God *in experience* (never in reality). Belief *is* experience for the believer, the only 'cure' being the dropping of belief and the lifting into God awareness. For the man and woman lifting into God

[1] Lao Tzu, *Tao Te Ching*   [2] Exodus 14:13

awareness, belief and its false sense of form dissolve and the love, harmony and wholeness of God become the formation of experience.

TRUE EXPERIENCE

True experience is no different from God because God is *all*, "and besides me there is none other." To material sense, experience seems incomplete, unjust, lacking unity, consisting of both good and bad causes and effects in every department of life. But to the spiritually aware, all is God—oneness, omnipresence, good without opposite—despite appearance. And so, in spiritual awareness, as you give of the infinity and omnipresence of resources to 'another,' what is truly happening, and what is literally and tangibly visible and real to you *if you recognize it*, is omnipresence 'giving' of itself 'to' itself in experience. In other words, in truth and actuality giving *is* receiving, and receiving *is* giving.

In conscious oneness, you are simultaneously the giver and the receiver. Oneness cannot give away some of itself, thereby leaving itself depleted of that thing or substance or amount. Where would it give it, other than to itself? And *what* would it give other than the whole of itself—which 'the recipient' already is and has? You see, to material belief, truth makes no sense, but to the consciousness of oneness, truth is the *only* sense.

Certainly, oneness *in experience* seems to include cause and effect, to give from 'here' to 'there,' but in truth and actuality 'here' and 'there' are the very same place of oneness and omnipresence, simultaneously *being and experiencing* all.

The whole of God—infinity—exists within, and is happening as individual being. Individual experience is the

measure of awareness we have of God being the truth and
actuality of all. This means that you *are* your whole world
of experience; you are one *with* and *as* experience. Nothing exists outside of, separate or different from your consciousness. You and your universe are one and
omnipresent, that oneness and omnipresence being consciousness. All is consciousness —the whole existing at
each and every point of itself simultaneously.

THE WHOLE IS ALWAYS PRESENT

Only the most miniscule fraction of infinity is visible
as objective experience at any moment, yet the whole is
always present. That tiny fraction appears as our entire
world and universe; yet, at each and every point of it, the
whole of infinity exists divinely invisible to objective
sense.

As one knows this almighty truth of self and world, infinity is 'released' as the reality of experience. Infinity of
all form becomes tangibly evident and freely available,
flowing moment-by-moment and step-by-step as the natural harmony and fulfillment of all experience. Without
knowing this truth, that which appears to be—good and
bad—is the limit of individual experience and ability. In
quantum physics this is referred to as the "anthropic principle"—that is, the only experience that can be perceived
by humans is the experience in which they exist (which
is that of, and the extent of, human intelligence and belief). This is why the Master instructed us to "Judge not
according to the appearance."

The truth is, infinity of all form and resource exists as
you and your world, and is fully and freely available exactly
where you are in experience this minute and eternally.

That which seems to be your and your world's 'lot,'

isn't—whether of good or bad health, wealth, relationship, opportunity, peace, morality, happiness, safety, security, justice or union. Whatever seems to be is not what, in and of its own self, actually *is*. What actually *is* is God, infinity and omnipresence—omni-oneness of all being, mind and formation. The forms of experience, being forms of consciousness, are fluid, not static, ever unfolding and expanding, ever new, fresh and more fulfilling. But we have to know this truth and live it in order to experience it.

When we know God to be the only reality, we forever *have* God, omnipresence and infinity at hand as the fulfilling experience of the world—our objective experience.

The point to realize is this: you are the very being, presence and form of infinity. Your entire world and universe is one with and as you. The universe and everything in it and of it is simply your magnified experience of consciousness. And because consciousness is God, which is infinity and omnipresence, the whole of God exists at every point of consciousness at the same time. Your entire experience and every point and place of it *is*, and is filled with the formation *of*, the infinity and omnipresence of God—good without opposite. "The earth is full of the goodness of God."

As you know and live this truth—the *one* truth—the windows of infinity are wide open wherever *you* are, making visible the true, good and fulfilling forms of earth; omnipotence and omniscience live within, and as, and all around you; the boundless good of God-being and God-formation is alive and vital as your *conscious* awareness; and infinity, inclusive of all its formation, is forever and freely yours to give, serve and share at every moment. Indeed, every moment is a moment of infinity, omnipresence, spirit and love, with one purpose of being: to unconditionally *give* of itself to all in its experience.

THE MORE YOU GIVE, THE MORE YOU HAVE

Do you see that in this consciousness, the more of infinity you *give*, the more your experience *has?* When you know that all is infinity, and you ceaselessly pour it out to the world, ever greater *amounts of* infinity in all good and fulfilling form are visible and spontaneously at hand.

'You' and 'your world' are one, not two, not different, not separate. Consciousness (God) is what 'you' and 'your world' are, and because consciousness *is* the infinitude itself—omnipresent at each point of itself simultaneously—infinity is literally, and in every real and practical way, fully available as each moment's form of fulfillment. Do you catch that?

We can use the cinema as an illustration. Let us assume the movie projector, its light, the reel of film and the screen are *one*—one organism or presence or being rather than four different and separate elements making up the experience of watching a movie. It is easy to see that if the projector somehow withheld its giving (projecting) of light through the film, there would be a lack of forms on the screen. But as the projector freely *gives* of its light through the reel of film, the screen is abundantly populated with images which form the whole and complete movie. As we understand all four elements of the experience to be *one*, we easily see that the giving and the receiving are also one—and experienced as such by the whole. The more the projector *gives*, the more it *has* in its world because it and the screen are one—not two, not separate or different.

This is the secret: the more that is given and received *is itself* the greater abundance of the whole experience— the magnifying or blossoming of infinity as all forms of experience.

Listen to the Master again. "Give, and it shall be given unto you; good measure, pressed down, and shaken together, and running over, shall men give into your bosom. For with the same measure that ye mete withal it shall be measured to you again."

The only individual who does not understand giving, or who is afraid or hesitant to give, is one who believes appearance to be real. But the Master tells us, "Do not judge according to the appearance, but judge righteous [truthful] judgment."[1]

In the consciousness of truth—of oneness, infinity and omnipresence—giving becomes our primary way and treasure of life. We know that infinity has only one thing to do in experience—to ceaselessly give of itself, that giving and receiving are one, and that giving *is* receiving. And because we are the presence of infinity, we *are* the giving and the receiving flow of experience.

We have awakened to the truth that our entire purpose and fulfillment of being have little to do with 'us' and 'our satisfaction,' but everything to do with giving, serving and sharing for the benefit of the whole *oneness* of experience.

"TWELVE BASKETS FULL LEFT OVER"

Giving *in the realization of,* and *as, oneness* infallibly 'gives back' more than is 'given.' Why? The minute you realize that infinity is omnipresent as all form, place and condition (even though undetected by material sense), and you begin giving out of that realization, infinity cannot help but 'give back' continually magnified amounts of itself.

You open the dam of infinity in the world of experience, and experience becomes flooded with all of infinity's form and wonder. You have awakened and now live with a new reality. The substance and form of the world

[1] John 7:24

has changed in your awareness from that of matter (false belief) to that of infinity (truth). In being aware of this truth, you are the 'outlet' of infinity to your experience and the experience of those in your presence. You watch your unconditional giving multiply and transform the "loaves and fishes" of the experience—the forms of health, wealth, harmony, peace and freedom.

Truth ever multiplies in experience. Giving in truth is not a one-for-one deal! It's a one for two, or three, or five, or ten, or one hundred times multiplying fact of truth. "He that heareth the word, and understandeth it, also beareth fruit, and bringeth forth, some an hundredfold, some sixty, some thirty."[1]

The act of giving *as all-inclusive oneness* is itself the "bearing fruit and bringing it forth," the revealing of the miracle of life everywhere present *as* wholesome, boundless, perfect, free and purposeful.

You do not give an 'amount' or a 'type' or 'category' of substance or form, even though objectively it may appear so. You give *God* as substance and form, *infinity* as substance and form, *omnipresence* as substance and form.

In the awareness of all-inclusive oneness, infinity and omnipresence—'inner' and 'outer' being the same one place, one environment, one being and one activity of infinity—the act of giving *is* the act of receiving. Because only oneness is, there is only *one* act or activity, and it is always whole and self-complete. God is *one*, not two or more, and that *one* is forever whole, complete and indivisible, incapable of being separated or disjoined.

GIVING *IS* RECEIVEING;
RECEIVING *IS* GIVING

Giving *is* receiving, and receiving *is* giving. The act of

[1] Matthew 13:23

giving instantaneously reveals a greater magnitude of infinity 'coming back.' The personal, finite, 'me and mine' sense is loosening and the true God sense (the giving sense of oneness and unity) is awakening and becoming more conscious of its true world filled with heavenly treasures. That greater measure of conscious awareness, and the giving, serving and sharing that accompany it, appear as the world generously or even abundantly giving back to the giver. Wherever you are and whatever you're doing, your world opens itself out in an omnipresent way, pouring back to you *your* giving consciousness and activity. In other words, the visible and tangible *quantity* of infinity becomes ever greater as the good forms of life. You discover your experience filled with the good and love, the wisdom and peace, the health and wealth, and the tenderness and grace of God.

This *appears* to material sense to be an individual giving to the world which, in turn, gives back to the individual. But the appearance is false, as all appearance is. "Judge not by the appearance." Nothing material is taking place. Only oneness is taking place, and oneness reveals ever magnified forms of itself *as it is given.*

It is like the magician drawing forth a score of objects from his hat—objects far too large in size and number to fit into a hat! Infinity reveals ceaselessly-multiplying good forms of itself as it is freely and selflessly given.

Giving in God consciousness draws forth (reveals) the infinity of God-form which is omnipresent at each and every point of experience—like the fullness of math or aerodynamics being present at each and every point of experience. Material sense cannot detect it, therefore does not believe its presence, or even its existence. But God-sense does not judge by belief or appearance. It judges only "righteous [truthful] judgment," and knows the infinity and omnipresence of God as all formation. In this consciousness, as it gives it receives because its whole world is *one* with, and as, it.

It makes perfect and logical sense that oneness can only give to itself, not to 'another.' No 'other' exists in oneness. The macro, multiplicity of experience is actually the micro oneness of I. "I am that I am."

OMNIPRESENT INFINITY OF ALL FORM

The entire infinity of good (God) without opposite exists fully manifested and demonstrated as, and at, every place of your universe. Your consciousness is your universe, your kingdom; your consciousness is the omnipresence and infinity of God.

Health, harmony, abundance and peace are everywhere without exception. The mind, body and earth are laden with God, and are God itself, plump with the fruits of truth and fully visible, tangible and real to experience. The spiritually aware individual needs just to *rest* in this awareness, unattached and unconcerned, simply observing God formation unfold as every he, she and it—as a flower unfolds her petals.

God is the truth of mind, body and earth and everything everywhere in and of earth. God is fulfillment, and so as material belief dissolves and spiritual awareness awakens and lives as individual being, God is experienced as fulfilling mind, body and earth and every form, activity and amount of earth. In other words, *truthful* mind, body and earth emerge as the fog of material belief dissolves, and all is witnessed as good and well.

It is all about *revealing that which already and forever is.* As we know and live the truth as best we each can, we have to begin to give, to pour out, to express, to serve and to share of our truth (infinity and omnipresence) of being. The Master gave us the secret: "Give, and it shall be given unto you; good measure, pressed down, and shaken together, and running over, shall men [the seeming 'outer'] give into your bosom. For with the same measure that ye mete withal it shall be measured to you again."

Malachi, in his breathtaking third chapter, also shares the 'result' of giving: "Prove me now herewith, saith the Lord of hosts, if I will not open you the windows of heaven, and pour you out a blessing, that there shall not be room enough to receive it."

Yes, I—omnipresent consciousness—will pour you out a blessing. I am the giving *and* the receiving—all *one;* I am the pouring out *and* the blessing 'coming back' so abundantly that there shall not be room to receive it—all *one.* I am the *one* which *is* the giving and the gift and which *is* the returning blessing and the recipient—*all one being and activity of giving, therefore revealing an ever magnifying experience of infinity.*

GIVING DOES NOT 'TRIGGER' RECEIVING

Do you see now? Giving *is* receiving; receiving *is* giving. Giving does not 'trigger' receiving. All is *one* and the *same act*, the *same presence.*

All is the same *one infinity of form*, revealing ever more of itself *as it is expressed.* The moment you realize this wondrous truth, giving becomes your primary and most fulfilling way of being. Giving, serving and sharing is the only truthful and fulfilling way of being, and the only way to behold the glories and bounties of God as mind, body and earth. Giving is the only way to awaken to your true talent and to successfully express it, and the only way to discover true love, joy and happiness.

As we give in the consciousness of oneness, we know our giving and our evidencing of the fruits of giving to be *revealed infinity.* The miracles of life and the multiplication of good form become tangibly evident *as and by the act of giving infinity.* The miracle of God on earth is not cause and effect; it is the *expressing,* the *giving,* the *pouring out,* the *sharing* of being, the very act of which *is the revealing* of ever more infinity.

To material sense, this looks as if good form is 'multiplied' (as in the multiplication of the loaves and fishes), or that ill health, disease or injury is 'healed,' or that lack and limitation is 'made prosperous,' or disagreement or war is 'pacified and harmonized.' But to awakened spiritual being, it is simply that the omnipresence of infinity becomes ever more evident to experience *as* the act of giving, and this is so.

UNDERSTAND THE MIRACLE OF ONENESS

Friends, take heed. Understand the miracle of oneness, the miracle of spiritual being, the miracle of *you,* your mind and earth, and *be* that miracle. Know and trust and *be* your truth. You are the infinity of being, of all things and all experiences.

Freely and ceaselessly pour forth the infinity of yourself in all ways 'intangible' and 'tangible,' realizing that actually all is *one,* not two; there is no actual 'intangible' versus 'tangible'; there is only oneness. Then watch the miracles that populate your world. Watch the miracle *you are being* become evident all over your experience. I can assure you that as you know the truth, and then get busy with giving as your primary way of being, nothing in the universe can stop or delay God from being evident throughout your mind, body and world.

This is why the Master told us, "Verily, verily, I say unto you, he that believeth on me [God as individual being, mind, body and earth], the works that I do shall he do also; and greater works than these shall he do."[1] It is *giving* as all-inclusive God presence, oneness, that evidences the miracle works of truth.

Understand this truth and *be it* by gently, yet ceaselessly and unconditionally, *giving* to all. Never go anywhere or do anything without *giving* some form of good. Never visit any person or place without *giving* some form of good to that person or place. Do not 'take' from person, place or condition, but forever *give* to every person, place or condition. 'Feed' him, her and it, 'supply' him, her and it, nourish and enrich him, her and it in some way and with some good and loving form—with some form of service, with a flower or bouquet of flowers, a note or card of love and appreciation, sweets or chocolates, food, fruit, cinema or theater tickets, a book or CD or DVD, dollars, a photograph or painting, a shirt or blouse or scarf. . . something, anything!

Most important of all, give of your *silence* and *receptivity*, your nothingness of personal, human self. Only when the personal sense of self is absent, is God in all its form present. The greatest gift of all is the gift of silence. In and through silence, God as being and as world is evident. It is by and through the *silence of your being* that you give the gift of life and happiness, love and union, abundance and success, joy and fulfillment.

Give the world your silence each and every day. You will call the 'result' a miracle.

I AND THE WORLD ARE ONE

The point is that in continually *giving* of your infinity

[1] John 14:12

of being, you continually *reveal* more of that infinity. "I am come that you may have life and that you may have it more abundantly."[1] The *I am come*—the spiritual *I* that awakens within, the truthful, peaceful *I* of being, body and world *felt* welling up and living within—has no purpose other than to *give of itself as the fulfillment of its world.*

I and the world are one and divinely purposeful. I—God as individual being, individual consciousness—does not live 'in' a world. I *is* its world, its universe. There is only one consciousness, God, and that consciousness is *the* infinitude, *the* omnipresence of itself being all. I 'and' consciousness are one; I *is* consciousness, consciousness *is* I.

Each body of consciousness—each individual being (you, me, all beings; the sons and daughters of God)—is the god of his or her world. "Ye are gods, and all of you are sons of the most High."[2] You are the god of your world, of your kingdom, of the entire body of you, your consciousness, and I am the god of mine. As the gods of our kingdoms, we ceaselessly *give* to each and every element of it, to each and every person, animal, plant, object, activity, amount, place and condition.

Our giving consists primarily of ceaseless recognition and realization of the *spiritual* identity of all, that *all is God, and besides God there is none other.* We then let God be our truthful world 'for us.' We feed and supply, relieve and comfort our world with *silence* which is its truth, its God, and which *is itself* the "image and likeness" of God as its formation. The presence of God—silence felt happening as our nothingness or transparency or window of self—fills the world of experience with spirit and truth, light and peace, harmony and joy, purpose and freedom. The more our world is fed 'by and through' our *silence of being,* the more the "image and likeness" of God is made evident

[1] John 10:10   [2] Psalm 82:6; John 10:34

as all formation. Silence released into the world of experience dissipates and dissolves the fog of material belief, revealing the *truth* of all mind, body and world.

GIVE FORM TOO

We give also of each and every *form* of fulfillment. We find that we can give without limit as we understand and live God's earth rather than 'our's.' "The earth is the Lords, and the fullness thereof; the world and they that dwell within"[1] and "The silver is mine, and the gold is mine, said the Lord."[2] As we understand and live this truth, we discover our experience filled with the boundless resources of all form. We feed and supply our world with the limitless dollars and opportunity, food and drink, clothing and shoes, home and shelter of God's earth.

"The earth is full of the goodness of God," and as the gods of God's earth we have the infinite and omnipresent resources of God ever at hand and ever tangibly available at every step and circumstance, place and condition.

In and as the *very act of giving*, the miraculous works of truth are revealed where untruth seemed to be. There is no limit to how 'much' of infinity and omnipresence and its forms we witness and are able to give as we know our and our world's spiritual identity. There is no limit to our freedom and fulfillment of being as we live in truth, released from belief, bind and condition. We are free in God and free to give to and serve our world without limit or hesitation imprisoning our expression.

OUR WORK THIS WEEK AND BEYOND

Immerse yourself in the reading and re-reading of this book. Ponder, slowly and deeply, each aspect of this spir-

[1] Psalm 24:1   [2] Haggai 2:8

itual clarity. Each chapter is a heavenly treasure, yours to freely take ownership of, then to tangibly witness as the miracle of truthful life—*your* life and the life of all, *your* world and the world of all, *your* purpose and fulfillment of being and that of all.

Start giving, pouring forth, and filling the world with the infinity of God you *are* and *have* in all its ways and all its forms. Give and give and give from the boundless resources of God *as* the god of your world. In so living, your being, mind, body and world fill with so much light that your seeing of God's good and harmony everywhere about is clear and sharp, never again to be fogged by belief in that which seems to be.

Never again 'take' from life. Taking from life is taking from yourself and your world of harmonious experience, thrusting your days into lack and limitation, discord and disharmony, pain and suffering. Taking is the dark and un-seeing of experience; giving is the light and clear-seeing of experience.

Give yourself and your world the gift of giving, the gift of God, the gift of life and love, light and peace, harmony and union—the gift of God's *silence* happening as you and your world. Silence is the greatest gift in the universe, the greatest treasure in heaven, the greatest purpose and fulfillment of being.

As you selflessly, unconditionally and ceaselessly give of your god-self, the light of truth shines throughout and ever more brightly and palpably as your mind, body and world. Mind, body and world defog to reveal their one truth. The world reacts, responds and opens its being to your truth, your recognition of its truth, and your giving to it. The world of "heaven as it is on earth" opens up and offers its glories and miracles to your experience and to the experience of everyone in your presence.

As you rest in the knowledge of all persons, animals, objects, activities, amounts, places and conditions being the very presence and form of God in experience, all opens wide its every window and door to you, pouring upon you its wealth of good. The whole world works as and for your fulfillment of purpose—that of giving the world the substance, light and food of truth—and supplies your every day and step with the omnipresent infinity of God-resource. "I am come that you [your entire being, mind, body and world] may have life, and have life more abundantly."

"DO YOU LOVE ME?"

In this way only can we look into the eyes of the Master and answer, "Yes" when he asks, "Do you love me?" You remember the Master's answer when the disciple Simon answered, Yes master, you know that I love you. "Then feed my sheep." Three times Jesus had to ask Simon the same question and three times Simon received the same answer, "Then feed my sheep." The disciple intellectually understood truth but hadn't yet awakened to his one true purpose and fulfillment, that of ceaseless giving to the world. Only as we awaken sufficiently to realize that *we are the gods of our experience*, and then begin to *be that god* by ceaseless giving—"feeding my sheep"—do we finally arrive at the glorious moment of *witnessing* God as all that mind, body and world is.

WITNESS GOD FILLING EARTH
WITH BLESSINGS

Truthful being is giving-being. There is no other truthful reason for being, and there is no greater truthful *act* than that of giving. Without giving to our kingdoms, we are empty and purposeless in truth. We cannot truthfully claim to love, seek and serve God with "all our heart, all our soul, all our mind, and all our strength," nor claim to truly be seeking spiritual awakening. And if not, we cannot be surprised that the promises and treasures of God are not ours in experience. Only as we love, seek and serve God with all that we are and all that we have do we witness God giving us (being evident as our experience) "the rain of your land in due season, the first rain and the latter rain, that thou mayest gather in thy corn, and thy wine, and thine oil."

Only in the tangible act of *being love*—of *giving* the gifts of love to the world—can we say to God: I love you. I truly am seeking truth by *being it* to the best of my hour-by-hour ability.

Indeed, "Give, and it shall be given unto you; good measure, pressed down, and shaken together, and running over, shall men give into your bosom. For with the same measure that ye mete withal it shall be measured to you again." The you that is 'giving' and the you that is being 'given unto' is the very *same you* experiencing the very *same act.* The oneness and omnipresence of being forever opens and reveals more of its infinity of good as we give in oneness, in wholeness and completeness, never wishing for a return or reward.

Giving *is* our return and reward, for all is one! In this realization, ever greater, richer, more bountiful and beautiful degrees of God as earth are witnessed. The forms of good and harmony, plenty and freedom multiply and fill the earth as we are *being* the good, harmony, plenty and freedom *by our giving.* The truth we each *are being* is the truth we each witness. "I am that I am."

We each *are* the individual infinity and omnipresence of God, and as we express that which we are, it is witnessed by that degree of expression.

"Verily, verily, I say unto you, he that believeth on me, the works that I do shall he do also; and greater works than these shall he do." This is the sacred key to heaven as it is on earth, the key to your highest and most wondrous truth and purpose.

This is the key which unlocks the deepest secrets and formations of God as your mind, body and world, unveiling heaven's immeasurable treasures, wonders and miracles to you and all within your presence.

~

My greatest prayer is that you will continue working with the messages in this book.

The more and more deeply you take them into your being, the more you will find yourself spiritually nourished and enriched, lifted and illuminated, seeking not the people and things of the world, but the peace, space, stillness and *silence* of God for the good and freedom of all beings, things and conditions of experience.

"As I be lifted up from the earth [from belief and false sense], I draw all men unto me."

MEDITATIONS

AND

WISDOMS

*Specific passages from the book
to meditate with and take
more deeply into being*

MEDITATIONS AND WISDOMS

WEEK ONE
THE FIRST TRUTH

"All things were made through him, and without him nothing was made that was made," and "God saw every thing that he had made, and, behold, it was very good."

"The earth is the Lord's, and the fullness thereof; the world, and they that dwell therein." Therefore "I am that I am."

"Unless the Lord builds the house, they labor in vain that build it; unless the Lord guards the city, the watchman stays awake in vain."

We must take truth *literally*. Truth must become a living, moving *reality* to us and as us. Truth must become what we are *in living awareness*.

Truth *is already* what we are, but because truth, God, the infinite, is *consciousness*, the entire 'secret' of awakening is *conscious awareness* of who and what we truly are and have—our spiritual identity. All is God: "All things were made through Him, and without Him nothing was made that was made."

The act of *awakening*—becoming *consciously aware* —is *itself* tangible and visible experience. There is no such thing as unembodied awareness.

There is no unmanifested or unembodied God, truth, awareness. God is fully manifest, fully embodied, infinitely so. "The place whereon you stand is holy [whole] ground."

What is God? "God is Spirit: and they that worship him must worship him in spirit and in truth."

Realize *your individual pondering, contemplating, keeping your mind on God* is the "taking root" of truth in your being and world.

MEDITATIONS
AND WISDOMS

WEEK TWO
TAKING THE FIRST TRUTH DEEPER

Miracles of truth begin to reveal themselves as we take the roots of truth more deeply into the spiritually en-riched soil of consciousness.

The more we are aware of omnipresence—of *one whole* rather than 'two' separate parts—the *more immediately the fulfillment of oneness* is experienced.

God is whole and complete; God is utterly finished and fulfilled, whole, complete, perfect.

The spiritual universe *is* before (meaning 'within,' not 'before' as in time) the universal *image* or *experience*.

Spiritual man is before the *image* of man (named 'mental and physical'); light fills the universe before the *image* of the sun is in the sky.

God *is* mind *is* form.

That which *is*, is an image and likeness of itself in or as experience—"the image and likeness of God."

The *very act* of pondering truth more and more deeply, the very act of forever expounding and substantiating our individual awareness of the great spiritual truths *is the revealing* of greater and richer tangible forms and activities of good in our experience.

God awareness *is* tangible experience.

All is one being, one happening, one form, one experience, never 'two,' never God or God-awareness *producing* or *manifesting* or eventually *becoming* produced, manifested, demonstrated, tangible and visible experience.

The only thing that ever presents itself to you is God.

Every 'he, she or it' is spirit and truth—"God is spirit: and they that worship him must worship him [recognize all] in spirit and in truth."

The more you 'spiritualize' your being, the more of the good formation of spirit you experience as everything everywhere of your world.

The truthful state of being is *peaceful, still, spacious, receptive and lives with an air of silence about it.* Therefore, only in and as *that state of being* can truth be evident.

The more spiritually peaceful, still and spacious you become, the more of peace, stillness and fulfillment you witness as your world because being and the forms of being—this world—are not separate, apart or different from each other, but are one.

Have plenty of silence (in and through which the "image and likeness" of God—good—becomes evident as formed experience).

MEDITATIONS
AND WISDOMS

God is *consciousness*.

God, truth, is the *one reality*—perfectly tangible and practical, and immediately so for those willing to sufficiently spiritualize their awareness.

The *all* that we name *God*—which is one hundred percent consciousness—exists utterly complete, manifested, demonstrated, tangible and visible as the whole of itself in perfect, intricately divine order (oneness) at every point of itself simultaneously.

There is no place or condition anywhere in infinity in which, or as which, God is lacking or not entirely visible and tangible, manifested and already demonstrated.

God is *the infinitude, the omnipresence, the oneness* of all, there being "none else," therefore leaving none out or lacking in the fullness of God.

There is no life but the whole of life itself (God, one-ness, eternity).

Belief in matter *is itself* the sense of separation from that which we truthfully are and have (the whole of God, infinity and omnipresence).

Because *belief is experience*, the *sense* of being separate and different from God leaves us imprisoned in an experience devoid of wholeness, completeness and freedom of being.

Consciousness (life, God, spirit, truth) does not have within it or as it—nor does it produce or form or become or change into—a material, physical body, form, object, amount, condition, circumstance, or activity.

Pure consciousness does not change its nature, substance, body, form, amount or activity, nor *can* it, nor would it have a reason to. *I am the only; only I exist; I am all, therefore only I am 'needed.'*

Realize the first three truths as meaning—

All things were (are) made through and as pure consciousness, and without pure consciousness nothing was (is) made that was (is) made.

Pure consciousness sees every thing that it has made, and behold, it is very good—very pure, made of pure consciousness.

God is pure consciousness: and they that worship him must worship him in the truth—the undeviating fact—that all is pure consciousness.

God, consciousness, is *silence.*

God form as earthly good, wholeness and harmony is experienced as and 'through' *silence.*

MEDITATIONS
AND WISDOMS

The earth is the Lord's and the fullness thereof.

Do you see that *all* is God? Do you see that there is not, and cannot ever be, an exception to this truth?

The only thing that exists is God; the only thing that can ever present itself to you is God, for there is—most literally—none else.

The 'earth'—which is unfortunately believed to be of matter (material and physical; corporeal)—is simply an earthly *sense* of spirit, a corporeal *sense* of that which is one hundred percent incorporeal.

The earth and everything everywhere in it and of it is nothing less than or different from the fullness (omnipresence) of God.

All *experience* is God, and is *of* God. What 'else' could experience be or consist of if all is God—which, indeed, all is?

All *being* is God. What 'else' could being be or consist of if all is God?

All *body, organ and function* is God. What 'else' could body, organ and function be or consist of if all is God?

All *thing* is God. What 'else' could anything be or consist of if all is God?

All *amount* is God. What 'else' could amount be or consist of if all is God?

All *activity* is God. What 'else' could activity be or consist of if all is God?

All *place* is God. What 'else' could place be or consist of if all is God?

All *condition and circumstance* is God. What 'else' could condition and circumstance be or consist of if all is God?

Only God is. No matter what we 'name God' (the infinitude of being and experience)—even the name 'earth'—it is still and only God, for there is literally, and in the most practical way, "none else."

All is God *being* that allness; all is the macro *being* the micro, the micro *being* the macro—indubitable omnipresence, oneness.

All is God *being* the fullness of itself, the completeness of itself, the oneness of itself, the harmony, peace, bliss of itself alone.

All is oneness *as itself alone,* there being none else, not even one other grain, atom or subatomic particle existent in the whole of the infinitude, but all one and one*ness*—self-complete, self-abundant, self-fulfilled at each and every point of itself at the same time.

The way all *appears to be* is not the way all *is.*

Only God, spirit and truth is despite the dim or foggy *sense* of mind, body and world we believe and entertain.

God is *one, universal, all, unconditioned*, and unconditionally present and *available* as the reality of experience to
and as and for all.

There is no unmanifested or undemonstrated, invisible
or intangible God. God is all, therefore is the only *is*, the
only presence and the only formation.

Whatever *is*, is infinity and omnipresence itself being
that which is, that being God—the *only* existence.

Because all is God, there is no personal self, nor personal thing.

You are impersonal being, not personal being.

You are the infinity of being and experience, not a finite being with finite experience.

Because "The earth is the Lord's and the fullness
thereof," you do not own anything—not even your mind,
your body—not even a single breath or step. All is God
and God's.

You *experience*. You do not *own*.

You are the guest of life, not the owner.

You are the guest of your body; you do not own it.
You are the guest of your love relationship; you do not
own him or her.

You are the guest of your home, your furniture and
furnishings, your electronics, your objects of art and play;

you do not own them.

You are the guest of money; you do not own it, nor can you earn it.

You are the guest of your job, career, business or practice; you do not own it.

You are the guest of your customers, clients, patients or students; you do not own them.

You are the guest of absolutely every person, thing, place, condition and activity in your universe. You own nothing because "The earth is the *Lord's* [not yours or mine] and the fullness thereof."

In releasing your sense of ownership of person, home, job, career, business, things, conditions, amounts, circumstances—everything of the personal sense of being—you free yourself as spiritual being.

Detach from all you sense as being 'yours.' Realize *all* as God and God's, not to be 'gained' or 'owned,' but humbly experienced and creatively and impartially shared.

It is in releasing ownership—that of the personal sense of life—that you free yourself and discover your experience filled with all that God is and has.

I am free in non-ownership, in the impersonal, universal, incorporeal truth of being, sharing all with all, unconditionally, impartially, each hour, each day.

Truth consciousness fills you, is you, and embraces you, supports you, lifts you, enriches you. Bathe in it many times throughout the day and night. Allow it to 'seek you' as you rest in its stillness, peace and completeness of being.

MEDITATIONS
AND WISDOMS

WEEK SIX
THE LOST BUDDHA AND CHRIST
CONSCIOUSNESS

There is a sublime state of being that sees through all appearance to truth. It has been referred to as the *healing consciousness.* More accurately stated, it is the *revealing* consciousness—the Buddha or Christ consciousness, that state of being that reveals, through the fog of 'human,' material belief, the infinity and omnipresence of God as all.

God *is.* Because God is the infinitude itself, omnipresent at and as each point of itself at the same time, it is clear that nothing 'else' other than the omnipresence of infinity *is,* or can be. Nothing 'else' exists and nothing 'else' can exist.

"Judge not according to the appearance, but judge righteous judgment."

The appearing he, she, it, place, activity, amount, circumstance or condition has no nature, quality or condition at all *in and of its own self.*

There is nothing but God (incorporeality, infinity and omnipresence) despite all and every apparent presence and experience—apparent reality.

Only truth is. Only one (God) and one*ness* (God experience) is—one life, one being, one body, one presence, one power, one intelligence, one nature, one quality and one condition. It is only *belief* and the troubled, attached-to-appearance, separated-from-God *sense* that obscures truthful experience.

Truth stands all around you this minute, filling your very world with good, completeness and harmony. The world is the God-world, the only world in existence—oneness and omnipresence, "earth as it is in heaven."

There is nothing real in or of appearance as it seems to be, therefore nothing real with which to engage, or 'do' something about, maintain, fix or heal in and of its own self. It is appearance (formation) only.

Appearance *in and of its own self* does not matter. It has no reality, no power, no quality, no truth. Leave it alone and be unattached to it in the realization that only God is.

Nothing of appearance (experience) in and of its own self is truth, nor can it of its own self evidence truth.

It is *illumined sense* that enables one to see the untouched and eternal truth of the body.

Appearance, because it *is* nothing but appearance, needs no more 'done' about it than images on the movie screen need something done about them.

Instantly realize that any and every appearance—the whole of it, including all its detail—'just is' and is therefore of no consequence. It has no power because only God is power. It has no quality because only God is quality. It has no body or form or amount or function because only God is body, form, amount and function.

Realize more deeply the non-reality of all appearance, all of experience *in and of its own self.*

Detach ever more from everything that appears to be, everything of experience, both 'good' and 'bad.'

MEDITATIONS
AND WISDOMS

WEEK SEVEN
CONSCIOUSNESS IS THE MIRACLE

"The earth" in our statement "The earth is the Lord's and the fullness thereof" means *consciousness.*

Everything, infinitely, is consciousness. Understand that, "consciousness is the Lord's and the fullness thereof."

Everything in and of individual consciousness, your consciousness and mine, everything, everything, *everything*—everything we can name and experience, without exception—is consciousness witnessed *as and being itself.*

Because God *is* mind *is* formation (earth and universe and every being and thing everywhere in it and of it, without exception), *all is God* and *of* God.

Nothing of God, mind or formation (earth) is anything but the *fullness* of God. Oh, if you can understand this you will walk right into your truth and freedom this day!

When we observe any and every him, her, it, activity, amount, place and condition, what we are observing is God and the fullness of God because there is nothing but God, therefore nothing but God to observe or experience: "He that sees me sees him that sent [is] me.... For in him we live, and move, and have our being."

Only when we add *belief* to experience do we suffer because belief about experience instantaneously separates us *in sense* from God.

Humanity has never understood that it itself— and its world and universe itself—is the very presence of God, oneness (because there is "none other"), simply experienced as conceptual mind formation.

Mind is God-mind because nothing other than God is; and because all formation is of mind, all formation is, and is as full of God as mind is.

What appears to be human *isn't;* it is God because only God is.

What appears to be finite *isn't;* it is infinity because only God, infinity is.

What appears to be local and separate *isn't;* it is the oneness of omnipresence because only God is and God is one and omnipresent.

What appears to be objectified, 'an object' *isn't;* it is simply objectified *sense* of omnipresence.

This awareness of *no consciousness being 'mine,' all consciousness being God, therefore God's* is a giant leap in awakening.

You have been searching for a miracle that you have believed will heal your life, yet the very consciousness you have been searching with *is itself the omnipresence of inexhaustible miracles*—the one great and unconditional miracle of God itself being everything you are, everything you have, and everything you experience—inclusive of the subject and object, activity and amount of your experience.

But how *aware* are you of the miracle of God as all?

There is no such thing as unexpressed, unmanifested, undemonstrated, invisible or intangible awareness. Awareness *is forever* expressed, manifest, demonstrated, visible and tangible.

Oneness is oneness! Omnipresence is omnipresence! There is *none else*. There is *nowhere else*.

All already *is* and 'has happened.' There is not God *and*. There is not a spiritual being and world *and* a material being and world which spirit somehow fills or heals or harmonizes or prospers or pacifies.

There is no matter; there is only spirit—God, spirit and truth. Remember until it radiates from your every cell and breath—we are simply having a material *sense* of that which is one hundred percent spirit. Sense does not, nor ever can, 'change' spirit into matter.

Whatever *degree* of awareness you *consciously have*—or

we can say, you are consciously *being*—*is itself* your manifest, tangible, visible experience.

"The place whereon you stand is holy (whole, omnipresent) ground." You are the *fullness* of God, the whole of infinity and omnipresence being itself as you and your world, *but* your versus my individual experience is entirely dependent on the degree of *conscious awareness of truth* we individually have, or *are being* moment-by-moment, hour-by-hour, day-by-day.

Individual consciousness *is* the miracle of God, and becomes perfectly visible and real for you and everyone to see wherever you let *it itself* live as you and every form of experience.

Truth does not 'show' in experience unless it is *being consciously and constantly realized.*

Awareness of truth *is* the visibility and tangibility—the reality—of truth in experience. This is the great key to the God-experienced life, to true spiritual awakening, to harmonious and purposeful being.

Ignore all appearance—both the seeming problem and its seeming solution—and *seek God, spirit, the "kingdom of heaven"* instead.

Seek the one reality, the one truth that exists here and now as everything everywhere of your consciousness.

It is *conscious awareness of God as all* that opens and reveals "the earth full of the goodness of God."

MEDITATIONS
AND WISDOMS

"I have food to eat of which you do not know."

My food is spirit *felt* welling up within, filling and fulfilling my experience of being.

My being is *tangibly fulfilled* as I sit still and silent, receptive to and being filled with spiritual experience—the *feeling* of God happening within me, as me. That feeling *is* the experience of fulfillment; the feeling *is itself* the fulfillment of being.

When we know this—really know it—and when we rely on the experience, *the feeling of spirit and truth happening within*, then our good is experienced as whatever form represents our current fulfillment.

"Do you not say, 'There are still four months and then comes the harvest'? Behold, I say to you, lift up your eyes and look at the fields, for they are already white for harvest!" Jesus is telling us not to assume there is a delay in spiritual fulfillment. Fulfillment is never delayed; fulfillment *is*.

God is spirit, and those who worship him must worship in spirit and truth. The true 'food' of life, the 'flesh,' the 'bread,' the 'wine,' the 'life,' the 'currency' of being is spirit and truth. *That* is the real presence, the real substance, the real body, the real form, the real food, the real amount, the real peace and harmony, justice, safety and security, the only only, the *one*, even though it *appears through the five senses to be* material or physical form, finite in nature, limited in amount, variable in quality.

Spirit and truth experienced 'happening' literally "feeds" the experience of body without material food.

If we continue to look out at the material scene and believe it, we enslave ourselves, including the forms of our experience, in the prison of that belief—in materiality and its laws, its methods, seasons, processes, its time and space, its pairs of good and bad opposites, of presence and absence. *Do you not say [believe], There are still four months and then comes the harvest? . . . Whoever drinks of this water [material belief] will thirst again*—for all the truth of life.

Whatever individual or collective being believes *is so* in its experience. Belief *is experience.*

Illumined (spiritual) being knows that the only true food—the only true fulfillment in and of any form and amount—is God, spirit and truth.

You need nothing other than *God-is-now* because there isn't anything but God as all, now. Therefore, when you have God *consciously living as all of your awareness*, you have the infinity and omnipresence of God formation everywhere you are, and as the resource for everything you do.

Material evidence is nothing but a state of dim or foggy belief veiling the whole and unconditional presence of God (fulfillment) as experience.

Lift up your senses! Lift up your awareness to God-alone-is!

Silence your sense of self many times throughout each day.

In the *silence* of being, I am.

In the *silence* of experience, I am fully visible.

MEDITATIONS AND WISDOMS

WEEK NINE
UNDER THE GOVERNMENT OF GOD

Just a blink away from your immediate comprehension is the true you living in the true world of spirit and peace, joy and harmony, love and purpose.

Every infinitesimal detail is in place, pre-prepared for you—*I prepare a place for you.... Before you call I will answer.*

Stop, be still, and *feel* the finished kingdom happening as you—the whole and complete, forever fulfilled kingdom of life happening as itself, as the life you are, and the body and world you experience.

Simply feel your *presence* happening, that's all.

Your presence is the *one* presence, God, omnipresence.

Feel its presence happening.

Feel its rhythm.

Feel its gentle pulse happening as you.

Feel its peace, its love, its grace happening as you.

Feel its silence. That silence is the truth of you, the oneness and completeness of you.

The silence *felt happening as you* is the greatest power on earth, your greatest gift of life and love to mankind, your greatest gift of peace, harmony and freedom to earth.

Nothing of God is hidden from tangible experience as *silence* lives you.

God *is* silence, silence *is* God.

"Be still, and know that I [the very I of you, the very consciousness, mind, body and world of you] am God."

Bathe in the presence of God, let the omnipresent light of love and grace flood you and fill you full, illumine all your senses so that you become aware of, and see, and have *conscious tangibility* of this world filled with God, spirit and truth.

Rest, relax, be still, be peaceful, be spacious, be receptive. Be attentively open to God happening as your entire 'you,' and *simply receive.* That's all.

Never judge by the appearance. *Nothing* of appearance, of its own self, is truth. Therefore ignore it.

Nothing that seems to be, is. Therefore nothing that seems to be 'good' is, and nothing that seems to be 'bad' is. Why judge, therefore? Why fret? Why worry? Why fear? Why react?

Why make effort to try to fix or pacify or heal or prosper the appearance?

Why struggle and strive to either improve the 'bad' things and conditions of appearance or gain more of the 'good?'

Judge by—sense by, react and respond to, rely on—truth *alone*, God *alone*, the presence and reality of spirit and truth *alone*.

All is God.

Nothing that exists, exists God-less. Everything that exists is the fullness of God as the form of experience. Nothing is without God, nothing lacks God, or is less than or different from God. All is God and the whole thereof. All is the very presence and mind-form of God itself, infinity and omnipresence itself.

God is, nothing 'else' is. Therefore, all is under the government of God, for there is no other presence, no other operating activity, law, principle or form.

Realize that *this very place* "on which you stand" is holy ground, whole and complete being, body, thing, activity, amount and condition—God itself and the "fullness thereof"—under the full government of itself, God, good, life, love, oneness and completeness of joy, harmony, peace and fulfillment of being in every way and as every form.

Let God *be* God *as* God *for* God as you, 'through' your

devotion to truth and your silence of being. In this way you are the 'outlet' of God on earth.

"By their fruits ye shall know them."

Only *tangible evidence* of God in experience is evidence that we are beginning to live by truthful identity, which is God as all.

We have to make ready our being so that, as and through spiritual awareness, spiritual (good and harmonious) formation becomes evident.

Belief in and attachment to matter clouds awareness. It is as if a dense fog exists throughout an individual's awareness leaving the world's one true and harmonious formation unclear or unseen, therefore unavailable in experience.

A God-aware (spiritually aware) and centered individual has a clear atmosphere of being, a clear and open consciousness that evidences the formation of itself, the "image and likeness of God."

Belief requires a believer or race of believers in which, and as which, to exist. You can see therefore, that as soon as the believer withdraws, all forms of belief equally drop away.

Only when we have sufficiently lifted our senses into God, filled or re-filled ourselves full of God awareness, is it possible to be really, really still and empty and silent, and in and as and through that stillness and silence, to feel the gentle presence of God happening as our being, body and world. God felt happening *is* the revealed God formation. The fog has been dissolved and God-formation emerges into plain sight.

Unless the Lord builds the house, they labor in vain who build it; Unless the Lord guards the city, the watchman stays awake in vain.

Do not make the mistake of assuming that truth-thinking (thinking about truth) can evidence truth, whereas non-truth thinking (thinking about matter) cannot. *No thinking*—truthful or non-truthful, even the most beautiful or poetic spiritual thinking—can evidence one cubit of truth itself.

Only God can evidence God.

God is happening as you and your entire world twenty-four hours day, but are you aware and attentive and receptive to it?

No matter where we are in our spiritual awakening,

God is always fully present and fully *tangibly available.*

Nothing else but *this* is the miracle of truth: the *consciously-experienced happening within*, with no effort on your part, no thinking it so, no making it so—just a still and silent openness and receptivity to that which is forever happening as your truth.

Be still, silent, attentive to, and expectant of "the Lord building your house," to truth *being* and revealing itself as your experience. Let consciousness itself *be* everything you are and everything you experience.

Nothing 'else' can because nothing 'else' is.

Nothing but God *felt* or *heard* happening within is God witnessed—God evidenced as formation.

Thinking does not make it so; knowledge about truth does not make it so; manipulating the mental, material or physical does not make it so. Only God is, and only God experienced—God felt happening within—is God *evident* as form.

The senses of being must be unattached and restful in God.

We must be still and attentive to spirit, a being of rest and peace, in order to feel the presence of God happening.

The kingdom of God, oneness, is the *only* kingdom—the *only* and *one* being, body, thing, place, amount, activity, world and universe.

There is no 'inner' versus 'outer.' The kingdom of God, oneness, is the *only* kingdom—the *only* and *one* being, body, thing, place, amount, activity, world and universe.

How wonderful and freeing to lose the false notion of 'within' versus 'without'! There never has been such division, such difference, such separation.

God *is* mind *is* formation.

Mind *is* formation. Nothing 'else' forms.

Form *is* mind; mind *is* form.

Forget completely the false idea of 'spirit' versus 'matter,' 'within' versus 'without,' 'God' versus 'humanity,' 'truth' versus 'world.'

> *When you make the two one, and when you make the inner as the outer and the outer as the inner and the above as the below, and when you make the male and the female into a single one, so that the male will not be male and the female not be female. . . then shall you enter the kingdom.*

All is one; therefore, experience is only of oneness. There is no other substance from which experience can be formed.

I live and move and have my being in God.

If a kingdom be divided against itself, that kingdom cannot stand. And if a house be divided against itself, that house cannot stand.

The only life, presence, power, body, form, amount and activity is God, spirit, truth. Therefore, the only *experience* is God, spirit, truth. There is none else.

When we feel God happening within, we *have* all of God as all of experience because the 'one' and the 'other' are actually the same *one* presence, the same *one* truth.

Nothing but *God experience happening as individual experience* is truthful experience.

Nothing we can think, know or do, either mentally, physically or materially, is truth itself; nor can *bring* truth into our experience.

Oh! If everyone could understand this profound statement of the Master! *I will not drink of the fruit of the vine, until the kingdom of God shall come.* The entire secret of awakened self is contained in these seventeen words.

"I will not [I am unable to] drink of the fruit of the vine [because there isn't yet any truthful fruit] until the kingdom of God shall come [shall be *felt happening as individual being and quickly witnessed as form*]." There it is, the whole secret!

As you make God-felt-happening your primary and most treasured daily activity, then the "life more abundant" becomes visible and real as your experience. *I am come that you may have life, and that you may have it more abundantly.*

Our work is not 'ours' but God's—truth's.

Rest, turn within, be still, attentive and receptive, and be patient while you "wait on the Lord."

Wait until you achieve sufficient stillness, silence and receptivity—seeking the experience of God for *its sake alone*, not for any reason of 'yours' or the 'world's'—until you *feel God happening, welling-up, stirring within.*

That alone is the miracle of you. That alone is truth evidenced. That alone is the 'healing.'

MEDITATIONS
AND WISDOMS

WEEK TWELVE
LIVING AS AWAKENED BEING

As we arrive at the wondrous state of *only-God-is* awareness—only omnipresence is, only allness, self-inclusive, self-contained oneness is—we have just one true purpose: to let "the Lord build the house," to let the kingdom of God be visible and tangible as our being and work, whatever that work may be.

A little more awake and alight in truth, we are aware that all appearance is nothing in and of its own self, and that God alone is the power and presence that dissolves the fog of false sense, revealing truthful sense and its "image and likeness" form. Indeed, "the battle is not yours, but God's."

And so we rest our senses. We settle down peacefully, receptive, relaxed, still; we become silent and receptive, relinquishing our entire sense and opening our being to God itself.

We make of ourselves a vessel for God, empty of thought and effort, silent, open and willing for God to *be* God *as* God *for* God as what appears to be us.

"And the wind ceased, and there was a great calm." The formed environment around us infallibly reveals itself to be the "image and likeness" of God—harmonious and peaceful—*when oneness is on the scene.* "Where the spirit of the Lord [oneness] is, there is liberty."

The "spirit of the Lord" is *God experienced happening* 'within' or as individual being.

The "manner of man" which all formation "obeys" is the *spiritual man,* the illumined consciousness of oneness.

The only identity in existence is God—spirit and truth—not God *and* matter; not God *and* human, animal, vegetable, object, amount, activity, place and condition.

Existence itself is all that exists—the *only,* the *whole* of existence existing at each point and place of itself simultaneously.

Wherever attention is placed, that 'place' is God experienced. When we know that, we are free in God as earth and its every treasure.

The more you know the truth and ignore appearance—accepting it as just appearance, not reality, not power, not any kind of body, function, amount, activity, character or condition of its own self, *remaining in, and being God consciousness*—the more you witness "the wind and the sea obey him [you]."

"And he will love thee, and bless thee, and multiply thee: he will also bless the fruit of thy womb, and the fruit of thy land, thy grain, and thy wine, and thine oil, the increase of thy cattle, and the flocks of thy sheep, in the land which he swore unto thy fathers to give thee."

The spiritually-recognized and -realized earth opens and gives all of herself to the spiritually-identified and -living individual. Why? That we can do the only thing that spirit does—ceaselessly, freely and unconditionally *give to* and *serve* our world of neighbors, colleagues, friends, customers, patients, students, strangers, places and conditions.

"Give, and it shall be given unto you; good measure, pressed down, and shaken together, and running over, shall men give into your bosom. For with the same measure that ye mete withal it shall be measured to you again."

After all is said and done, the only human malady is a lack of giving.

We cannot witness a single grain of God until we are *being* God being instead of 'human' being. To witness the one consciousness as all form—the so-called intangible, transcendental, incorporeal, the kingdom of heaven and its treasures on earth—we have to *be* and *give it, pour it out, release it.*

Life must consist of *outflow* not *inflow.*

In God, in oneness, in omnipresence, 'giving' and 'receiving' is one and the same action. Oneness pours forth *from all over itself simultaneously* and *gives back* from all over itself simultaneously.

In the omnipresence of oneness, where could there exist a *cause* which triggers a different existence named an *effect?* Where would or could there exist a *giving inner* that triggers a *giving back outer?*

Experience is different *only if we believe it to be.*

Belief separates us from God *in experience* (never in reality). Belief *is* experience for the believer, the only 'cure' being the dropping of belief and the lifting into God awareness.

True experience is no different from God because God is *all.*

Giving *is* receiving, and receiving *is* giving.

That which seems to be your and your world's 'lot,' *isn't.*

Whatever seems to be is not what, in and of its own self, actually *is.* What actually *is* is God, infinity and omnipresence—omni-oneness of all being, mind and formation.

Do you see that in this consciousness, the more of infinity you *give,* the more your experience *has?*

The only individual who does not understand giving, or who is afraid or hesitant to give, is one who believes appearance to be real.

Giving *in the realization of,* and *as, oneness* infallibly 'gives back' more than is 'given.'

The act of giving *as all-inclusive oneness* is itself the "bearing fruit and bringing it forth," the revealing of the miracle of life everywhere present *as* wholesome, boundless, perfect, free and purposeful.

Material sense cannot detect it, therefore does not believe its presence, or even its existence. But God-sense does not judge by belief or appearance. It judges only "righteous [truthful] judgment," and knows the infinity and omnipresence of God as all formation. In this consciousness, as it gives it receives because its whole world is *one* with, and as, it.

It is all about *revealing that which already and forever is.*

I am the giving *and* the receiving—all *one.*

Giving does not 'trigger' receiving. All is *one* and the *same act,* the *same presence.*

All is the same *one infinity of form,* revealing ever more of itself *as it is expressed.*

Understand the miracle of oneness, the miracle of spiritual being, the miracle of *you,* your mind and earth, and *be* that miracle.

Freely and ceaselessly pour forth the infinity of yourself in all ways 'intangible' and 'tangible,' realizing that actually all is *one,* not two.

Most important of all, give of your *silence* and *receptivity.*

The greatest gift of all is the gift of silence.

Give the world your silence each and every day. Your world will call the 'result' a miracle.

The more our world is fed 'by and through' our *silence of being*, the more the "image and likeness" of God is made evident as all formation.

Silence released into the world of experience dissipates and dissolves the fog of material belief, revealing the *truth* of all mind, body and world.

In and as the *very act of giving*, the miraculous works of truth are revealed where untruth seemed to be.

Never again 'take' from life.

Give yourself and your world the gift of giving, the gift of God, the gift of life and love, light and peace—the gift of *silence*.

Silence is the greatest gift in the universe, the greatest treasure in heaven, the greatest purpose and fulfillment of being, the greatest 'healing' influence.

TWO NEW MIRACLE SELF BOOKS

One, Feb 26, 2016
by Paul F. Gorman
$12.95 (Paperback, 140 pages)

One, the new book from Paul F. Gorman, author of The Miracle Self, offers a clear spiritual insight and meditation practice that enables the devoted spiritual aspirant to lift into the consciousness of oneness, and thereby quickly watch the flow of harmony open up in practical experience.

It is by today well known that in God consciousness—the consciousnesss of One—healing takes place. But what exactly is the consciousness of One? How exactly is it attained? Can the "average" or even new spiritual student achieve it?

One stands apart by lifting the reader away from material consciousness (which is all that distorts the one reality of health, abundance, harmony and peace from being experienced) into the consciousness of oneness where all good is visible, real and practical, and where sickness, lack and limitation dissolve.

Spiritual Healing of the Mind and Body, Sep 27, 2015
by Paul F. Gorman
$21.95 (Paperback, 268 pages)

Spiritual healing is real and practical, accessible by every person on earth. It is painless and without procedure; quick and powerful; frequently instant. Yet the law of spiritual healing —first given to the world around 460 BC by Gautama the Buddha, then around 2000 years ago by Jesus the Christ—is understood and practiced by only a handful of illumined individuals of each generation. The few who have it today freely and unconditionally give the gift of health and wholeness to all who come to them for help.

The great truth of humanity's spiritual identity and of the spiritual actuality of the mind and body exists—fully real and practical—in every individual. Yet, to most, it, like a hidden treasure, lies unknown within. From the moment an individual awakens to even a measure of spiritual light, the treasure of life is "released" and begins to flow into tangible form, quickly healing the body. "I am come that ye may have life, and have it more abundantly."

CPSIA information can be obtained
at www.ICGtesting.com
Printed in the USA
FSOW02n2003161116
27494FS